Rapture, The Bride Redeemed

Paul Lehr

Table of Contents

Chapter 1
Rapture???

Word Study

To the critic who says the word "rapture" is not in the English translation of the Bible. Congratulations to the critic, you are correct. The word "rapture" is not in the English translated Bible. Hopefully this does not shake anyone's faith. So where does the word "rapture" come?

For the answer, we have to go back to the fourth century. St. Jerome was commissioned by Pope Damasus in 382 AD to translate the Bible into the Latin language. St. Jerome translated the New Testament from the original Greek. The saint was the Pope's secretary. He finished the translation before Damasus died in 384 AD. After the Pope's death, St. Jerome moved to Bethlehem. By 405 AD, he had translated the Hebrew Bible or what we call the Old Testament. By the 13th century, St. Jerome's translation had become the official Latin translation of the Bible for the Roman Catholic Church. The Latin translation of the Bible is called the Vulgate. The Vulgate is generally credited as the first translation of the Old Testament. www.Vulgate.org

This is how we get our Bible. Depending on the version or translation we read, the New Testament was translated from the original Greek. The Old Testament was by in large translated from the Hebrew language with the exception of a few chapters in **Daniel** and **Ezra** which are written in Aramaic. Sorry, the Bible was not originally commissioned and written in Old English from the King of England in the early 17th century.

The example for the word "rapture" comes from **1 Thessalonians 4:17.** Jerome translated from the original Greek as written by the Apostle Paul. Below is the original Greek writing of the verse. The word in question is underlined in the Latin, Greek, and English versions.

1 Thessalonians 4:17 ἔπειτα ἡμεῖς οἱ ζῶντες οἱ περιλειπόμενοι ἅμα σὺν αὐτοῖς ἁρπαγησόμεθα ἐν νεφέλαις εἰς ἀπάντησιν τοῦκυρίου εἰς ἀέρα· καὶ οὕτως πάντοτε σὺν κυρίῳ ἐσόμεθα. https://net.bible.org/#!bible/1+Thessalonians+4

Epistula Ad Thessalonicenses I - Chapter 4:17 deinde nos qui vivimus qui relinquimur simul <u>rapiemur</u> cum illis in nubibus obviam Domino in aera et sic semper cum Domino erimus.

The word is "**rapiemur**" in Latin. www.Vulgate.org

1 Thessalonians 4:17 Then we who are alive and remain will be <u>caught up</u> together with them in the clouds to meet the Lord in the air, and so we shall always be with the Lord. New American Standard Bible.

The English word "rapture" comes from "rapiemur" of the Latin translation of the Bible.

1 Thessalonians 4:17 Then we who are alive and remain will be caught up together with them in the clouds to meet the Lord in the air, and so we shall always be with the Lord. The original Greek word for "caught up" is ηαρπαζο/**harpazo**. Per Strong's Concordance it means: to seize, carry off by force, claim for one's self eagerly, to snatch out or away.

Jesus will seize and claim eagerly for Himself those who believe in Him. Once believers are claimed, we are forever with Him. If the security of that verse is not enough…

The Greek word "harpazo" is used twice in **John 10:28-29.** This is Jesus talking in the two verses below. This time the term "harpazo" is translated as "snatch".

John 10:28-29 and I give eternal life to them, and they will never perish; and no one <u>will snatch</u> them out of My hand. My Father, who has given *them* **to Me, is greater than all; and no one is able <u>to snatch</u>** *them* **out of the Father's hand.** -Jesus

Once we are taken, believers have double coverage. Jesus Himself will securely protect a believer. By the Son's admission, the Father is greater and He has hold of those who believe as well. We are not going anywhere but with God. To quote the verses above, we **will never perish.** Talk about eternal security.

The Father and the Son know to "snatch" the believer because the individual is sealed with the Spirit.

Ephesians 1:13-14 In Him, you also, after listening to the message of truth, the gospel of your salvation—having also believed, you were sealed in Him with the Holy Spirit of promise, who is given as a pledge of our inheritance, with a view to the redemption of *God's own* possession, to the praise of His glory.

We have eternal security in the triune God. All three persons of the Godhead (Father, Son, and Spirit) are involved with the term "harpazo". We are "harpazoed" and property of God. Believers are not going anywhere but with God and into the clouds.

Seriously, can we realistically propel and sustain ourselves into the clouds? Talk about hang time... Are we capable of locating Jesus in the clouds? Over what city? How high is He suspended over the Earth? What time is the meeting?

We are helpless to achieve this concept on our own, as well as many others, apart from Christ. We are raptured, harpazo, caught up, rapiemur, or snatched. Take your pick. Just believe.

Chapter 2
The Gospel of Jesus Christ

There are primarily three perspectives in regards to the time when the rapture of the church occurs relative to the seven year tribulation or the Day of the Lord. The first is called a pre tribulation rapture (rapture before). The second is called a mid-tribulation rapture (rapture in the middle). And the third is a post tribulation rapture (rapture after). Now there will be more discussion regarding these positions and others later.

These three perspectives are hotly contested, debated, and divisive. As members of the body of Christ, we need to think about how we present ourselves to an unbelieving world and to other members of the church. Are our discussions and actions inviting? Would others want to join us? Are we a distraction or a barrier to others getting to know Jesus?

The discussion of "when" this event takes place has no bearing on one's salvation and eternal destination. People who hold to any of these positions and believe that Christ died for sins, was buried, and was resurrected…Heaven bound. All three rapture positions are likely members of the body of Christ.

A pastor I know has made a common sense statement, "Good men can respectfully disagree."

But, what is of the utmost importance is stated by the Apostle Paul. This is the priority. As believers in Jesus Christ we should draw a line in the sand and stick a flag in the ground over this issue. If a person does not get the issue of the gospel of Jesus Christ right, they have bigger trouble than the timing of the rapture.

1 Corinthians 15:1-4 Now, brothers, I want to remind you of the gospel I preached to you, which you received and on which you have taken your stand by which also you are saved, if you hold fast the word which I preached to you, unless you believed in vain. *For I delivered to you as of first importance* what I also received, that Christ died for our sins according to the

Scriptures, and that He was buried, and that He was raised on the third day according to the Scriptures…

Jesus Christ died. He was buried. And He was raised.

This is the gospel message of Jesus Christ. The gospel is the ευαγγελιον/euaggelion. This is really "good news".

Here is how Strong's Concordance defines "gospel". It is the glad tidings of salvation through Christ. This is the proclamation of the grace of God manifest and pledged in Christ. As the messianic rank of Jesus was proved by his words, his deeds, and his death, the narrative of the sayings, deeds, and death of Jesus Christ came to be called the gospel or glad tidings.

The resume of Christ is sequentially ordered in Strong's definition of the gospel. The glad tidings of the kingdom of God soon to be set up, subsequently also of Jesus the Messiah, the founder of this kingdom. After the death of Christ, the term comprises also the preaching of (concerning) Jesus Christ as having suffered death on the cross to procure eternal salvation for the men in the kingdom of God, but as restored to life and exalted to the right hand of God in heaven, thence to return in majesty to consummate the kingdom of God.

The issue of the gospel is not an intellectual decision. The gospel is a moral issue. Does God exist and does He take the issue of sin seriously? If so, then there is accountability. The issue needs serious attention. Eternal life and eternal death are on the line. The destination of your eternal soul is at stake. This is about getting your heart, mind, and soul right with the Creator.

This good news is for everybody! God does not discriminate. The most brutal, unsavory character can be saved from eternal hell if they believe the gospel message. One can think up the vilest person in their mind and that person too can be saved with their belief in Jesus Christ. We are all equal at the foot of the cross. Even a barbaric Scythian can be saved by the cross work of Jesus…

Colossians 3:11 *a renewal* **in which there is no** *distinction between* **Greek and Jew, circumcised and uncircumcised, barbarian, Scythian, slave and freeman, but Christ is all, and in all.**

Jesus Christ knew His destiny before the creation of the world. His death on the cross was planned before the Earth was formed. The three verses below will hurt your head when you stop and think about them.

Revelation 13:8 All who dwell on the earth will worship him, *everyone* whose name has not been written from the foundation of the world in the book of life of the Lamb who has been slain.

1 Peter 1:20a For He was foreknown before the foundation of the world...

2 Timothy 1:9 He has saved us and called us with a holy calling, not because of our own works, but by His own purpose and by the grace He granted us in Christ Jesus before time eternal.

Believers in Christ were chosen before the world was made. This does not mean we do not have free will. God is a gentleman. He does not force Himself on us. God does not want a robot. He wants our heart and free choice. He wants to be chosen. The first four commandments of the Ten Commandments imply we have a choice whether we worship God or not. A consequence is stated but God does not make us do anything. He knows what we are going to do and the choices we will make. He gives us that freedom.

Ephesians 1:4 just as He chose us in Him before the foundation of the world, that we would be holy and blameless before Him. In love...

God knows all and He is across the scope of time. He has always known us even before our lives on earth start. He even knows how long we are going to live. He has it covered.

Jeremiah 1:5 "Before I formed you in the womb I knew you, and before you were born I consecrated you; I have appointed you a prophet to the nations."

Psalm 139:14-16 I will give thanks to You, for I am fearfully and wonderfully made; wonderful are Your works, and my soul knows it very well. My frame was not hidden from You, when I was made in secret, and skillfully wrought in the depths of the earth; Your eyes have seen my unformed substance; and in Your

book were all written the days that were ordained for me, when as yet there was not one of them.

At the core of the need for the gospel message is a simple legal argument and matter. God made this very clear from the beginning of time in the Garden of Eden. Listen and obey God's directions. "Eat all you want except for one." There are consequences. Some are good and some are bad.

Genesis 2:16-17 The Lord God commanded the man, saying, "From any tree of the garden you may eat freely; but from the tree of the knowledge of good and evil you shall not eat, for in the day that you eat from it <u>you will surely die</u>."

As time progressed, Moses was given the Law for the nation of Israel on Mount Sinai. God communicated His Law to Moses approximately 3,600 years ago. These directions were given to Moses approximately 1,600 years before Christ. In total, there were 613 laws given. This number includes the Ten Commandments. Jews have even broken down the number of negative and positive commands. 365 are negative commands and 248 are positive commands. Read the first five books (**Genesis, Exodus, Leviticus, Numbers,** and **Deuteronomy**) of the Bible for these laws or mitzvoth (Hebrew term).

As far as God is concerned, there is no separation of moral and legal code. Culturally and legally the United States is different. We have a separation of church and state. That is not the case with God and His nation Israel.

Well so what if we break God's Law? What is the big deal? Sin is a big deal to God. It does not matter the offense. If you break the law, the punishment is death. It does not matter if one steals, lies, commits murder or adultery, covets, or whatever. There are no "shades of grey" when it comes to sin. There is not a sliding scale for sin. One sin is not more condemning than another. If you break one, you break them all. That is God's standard.

James 2:10 For whoever keeps the whole law and yet stumbles in one point, he has become guilty of all.

Romans 6:23a For the wages of sin is death…

1 Corinthians 15:56 The sting of death is sin, and the power of sin is the law…

The critic often says, "Well, the Ten Commandments are in the Old Testament and we live during the church age in the New Testament. Jesus took care of the Law."

A message for the critic, the Mosaic Law is still present whether you believe it or not. The issue is whether or not you have Jesus to cover your mess. The Mosaic Law and the Ten Commandments have not gone away. Jesus Himself made this very clear.

Matthew 5:17 "Do not think that I have come to abolish the Law or the Prophets; I have not come to abolish them but to fulfill them."

If we are at all honest with ourselves, we have some serious issues. The Mosaic Law has incredible standards. Who are we kidding! In our current state of humanity, we are all guilty. Adam introduced sin to humanity. The result was bodily death.

Romans 5:12 Therefore, just as through one man sin entered into the world, and death through sin, and so death spread to all men, because all sinned…

1 Corinthians 15:22 For as in Adam all die, so also in Christ all will be made alive.

Sin is the reason for illness and death. We don't know when or how we are going to die. But we do know the reason for death, sin. Missing the mark or missing the moral standard is the reason we sweat for crying out loud. Weeds were not supposed to grow. A rose was not intended to have thorns. We were not originally created for hard labor.

So the next time somebody asks, "Why does God allows bad things to happen? How could a loving God let that horrible thing occur?"

We need to take a long, hard look in the mirror and get real honest. Sin is why bad and evil things happen.

Genesis 3:17-19 Then to Adam He said, "Because you have listened to the voice of your wife, and have eaten from the tree about which I commanded you, saying, 'You shall not eat from it'; cursed is the ground because of you; in toil you will eat of it all the days of your life. Both thorns and thistles it shall grow for you; and you will eat the plants of the field; by the sweat of your face you will eat bread, till you return to the ground, because from it you were taken; for you are dust, and to dust you shall return."

As individuals, it is not our place to judge others regardless of their actions. Every person on the planet has a lifestyle or mental attitude issue that can be taken to task. There is no sliding scale or grading on the curve when it comes to sin. "Well my sin is not as bad as…" Nonsense, judgment belongs to God.

James 4:12 There is *only* one Lawgiver and Judge, the One who is able to save and to destroy; but who are you who judge your neighbor?

We are all in need of sin remission. Every single one of us is a sinner. We all have sin in our lives.

Ecclesiastes 7:20 Indeed, there is not a righteous man on earth who continually does good and who never sins.

Romans 3:23 for all have sinned and fall short of the glory of God…

We all (except a group of believers at the rapture) have a set time and date with the grave. It does not matter what our bodies look like. One cannot diet, vitamin, or exercise their way from the Pit. It does not matter if you are rich or poor. One cannot buy their way out of Sheol.

Psalm 89:48 What man can live and not see death? Can he deliver his soul from the power of Sheol? Selah.

Psalm 49:14 As sheep they are appointed for Sheol; death shall be their shepherd; and the upright shall rule over them in the morning, and their form shall be for Sheol to consume so that they have no habitation.

Job 26:6 Naked is Sheol before Him, and Abaddon has no covering.

The meaning of Abaddon is "destruction". Sin is naked awareness before God. In the final analysis, there is no covering of sin apart from the cross work of Christ. God has always made provision for the sin of humanity. Apart from God, sin will be exposed, bare, and raw. Its path leads to destruction.

Proverbs 15:11 Sheol and Abaddon *lie open* before the LORD, How much more the hearts of men!

Death is knocking. The open throat and grave of death await.

All Rise…And you have entered the Eternal Heavenly court room. God the Father is presiding over the court.

You have died. So how do you plead? Innocent or guilty. It is a loaded question, you are dead. Satan is the prosecution. There is a defense attorney provided for you if you accept His counsel. The defense attorney provided is offering free services if you are accepting. He will defend you free of charge. He is at your service if you believe He can do the job.

Your life is on trial. You will be judged by your actions. It is stated twice in **Revelation 20**, you will be judged by your deeds. Be careful what you ask for. There is a written record.

Revelation 20:12-13 And I saw the dead, the great and the small, standing before the throne, and books were opened; and another book was opened, which is *the book* of life; and the dead were judged from the <u>things which were written in the books, according to their deeds</u>. And the sea gave up the dead which were in it, and death and Hades gave up the dead which were in

them; and they were judged, <u>every one</u> *of them* <u>according to their deeds.</u>

It is important to understand and know your prosecutor. His name is Satan. He has a significant history of pointing out the sins of humanity. As a prosecutor, he never rests.

Revelation 12:10 Then I heard a loud voice in heaven, saying, "Now the salvation, and the power, and the kingdom of our God and the authority of His Christ have come, for the <u>accuser</u> of our brethren has been thrown down, he who <u>accuses</u> them before our God <u>day and night</u>.

This is hardly a fair trial. We know Satan is a prosecuting attorney from multiple sources in the Bible in both the Old and New Testament. Granted, we are guilty. But he is a tattletale all of the time and a very effective prosecutor.

Zechariah 3:1 Then he showed me Joshua the high priest standing before the angel of the LORD, and Satan standing at his right hand to <u>accuse</u> him.

Some would ask the question. Who is in charge Satan or God? At times, God will allow Satan to test people with limits. God grants that authority to Satan with **Job**. Satan knows who is in charge. When God calls, Satan comes. See **Job 2** for a detailed account of a conversation with Satan and God.

Job 2:6 So the LORD said to Satan, "Behold, he is in your power, only spare his life."

God is still in charge.

Revelation 2:10b …Behold, the devil is about to cast some of you into prison, so that you will be tested…

Satan is going to "test" and it is the Greek word πειραζο/**peirazo.** It is defined as: to test one maliciously, craftily to put to the proof his feelings or judgments; to try or test one's faith, virtue, character, by enticement to sin, tempt. -Strong's Concordance

When bad things happen it may or may not be Satan. Job never knew the source of his angst. Sometimes it is us that is the source of our issues.

God the Father is the presiding judge. He is absolutely holy and perfect in justice. There will be no plea bargain.

Psalm 89:14 <u>Righteousness and justice are the foundation of Your throne</u>; lovingkindness and truth go before You.

Psalm 97:2 Clouds and thick darkness surround Him; <u>righteousness and justice are the foundation of His throne.</u>

God cannot stand sin. He hates sin and His character demands that sin is punished, no exceptions.

Psalm 7:11 God is a righteous judge, and a God who has indignation every day.

Psalm 5:5 The boastful shall not stand before Your eyes; You hate all who do iniquity.

God cannot be bought or bribed. It does not matter how deep your pockets are. You don't have enough money or material possessions. Justice will be served.

Proverbs 11:4 <u>Riches do not profit</u> in the day of wrath, but righteousness delivers from death.

Zephaniah 1:18 <u>Neither their silver nor their gold will be able to deliver them</u> on the day of the LORD'S wrath; and all the earth will be devoured In the fire of His jealousy, for He will make a complete end, indeed a terrifying one, of all the inhabitants of the earth.

Community service is not an option. One cannot work away their crime and sentence. One cannot earn their way to God. Humanity is not going to work their way to Heaven.

Romans 3:28 For we maintain that a man is justified by faith <u>apart from works</u> of the Law.

2 Timothy 1:9 He has saved us and called us with a holy calling, not because of our own works, but by His own purpose and by the grace He granted us in Christ Jesus before time eternal.

Titus 3:5 He saved us, not by the righteous deeds we had done, but according to His mercy, through the washing of new birth and renewal by the Holy Spirit.

Ephesians 2:8-9 For by grace you have been saved through faith; and that not of yourselves, it is the gift of God; not as a result of works, so that no one may boast.

God the Father accepts only one payment for sin, the shedding of sinless blood on behalf of the guilty. Sinless blood is the currency of God. This concept of sinless blood covering sin starts back in the Garden of Eden. An animal or animals made in perfection during creation were sacrificed and skinned to allow for Adam and Eve to be clothed or covered. Clothing is a reminder of sin.

Genesis 3:21 The LORD God made garments of skin for Adam and his wife, and clothed them.

We were created naked and it was not a big deal. But, all of that changed when sin was introduced to the creation.

Genesis 2:25 And the man and his wife were both naked and were not ashamed.

Dollars, Pounds, Shekels, and precious metals do not count in God's economy. They are not acceptable currency.

1 Peter 1:18…knowing that you were not redeemed with perishable things like silver or gold from your futile way of life inherited from your forefathers…

There is no way any of us qualify for the standard of sinless blood. None of us are sinless. We are all guilty.

Romans 3:23 for all have sinned and fall short of the glory of God…

Fortunately it is not up to us to provide our own solution for our sins (even though some of us think we have the solution). God the Father has a provision for sin. He has the definitive option and an adequate payment plan. There is only one way. The plan involves His Son.

Isaiah 9:6…a son will be given to us…

The purpose of the Son is clarified in **John 3:16.**

John 3:16 For God so loved the world, that He gave His only begotten Son, that whoever believes in Him shall not perish, but have eternal life.

This fact in history has binding results today and into the future. The grammar of the verse (**Isaiah 9:6**) in Hebrew indicates that the Son is given to us, a gift.

Yes, we are guilty. But God the Father offers us a free gift. Somebody has taken our fine and paid it for us. He has paid our debt without charging us.

Romans 6:23 For the wages of sin is death, but the free gift of God is eternal life in Christ Jesus our Lord.

And this is where the mercy, grace, and forgiveness of Jesus enters the scene. Christ loves us <u>ALL</u> in spite of our actions whatever they may be. He paid the penalty for sin. For those who believe, He has paid the fine for sin. Jesus Christ is our answer and defense.

Jesus is without sin and led a sinless life. He is a qualified defense attorney. He is able to pay the fine for sin. Based on His sinless life, He is able to die and shed sinless blood.

2 Corinthians 5:21 He made Him who knew no sin to be sin on our behalf, so that we might become the righteousness of God in Him.

1 John 3:5 You know that He appeared in order to take away sins; and in Him there is no sin.

1 Peter 2:22 He committed no sin, neither was deceit found in his mouth. Peter is quoting Isaiah 53.

It is the shedding of Christ's blood that is the forgiveness of sins. The Old Testament sacrificial system does not apply. Animal sacrifices do not ultimately pay for sin. Animal sacrifices were object lessons pointing toward the ultimate sacrifice, Jesus Christ.

Hebrews 9:12 He (Jesus) entered once for all into the holy places, not by means of the blood of goats and calves but by means of his own blood, thus securing an eternal redemption.

An Old Testament example that foreshadowed the coming of Jesus is the mercy seat on the Ark of the Covenant. His character was prophesied in the famous Temple artifact. The mercy seat is the cover or lid for the Ark of the Covenant.

Exodus 25:17 You shall make a <u>mercy seat</u> of pure gold, two and a half cubits long and one and a half cubits wide.

The Hebrew word for "mercy seat" is **kapporeth**. Per Strong's Concordance it means: mercy seat, place of atonement; the golden plate of propitiation on which the High Priest sprinkled the seat seven times on the Day of Atonement symbolically reconciling Jehovah and His chosen people; on the lid were two golden cherubim facing each other whose outstretched wings came together.

The Hebrew word **kapporeth** comes from **kopher** (means propitiatory or substitution).

The mercy seat or the lid of the Ark is a substitution for the covering of sin.

For God, the shedding of innocent blood on the mercy seat is a satisfactory substitution for sin. Only the High Priest can make the sacrifice in the presence of God.

Jesus is our High Priest who sacrificed His blood for sin.

Hebrews 4:14 Therefore, since we have a great high priest who has passed through the heavens, Jesus the Son of God, let us hold fast our confession.

Jesus Christ is the mercy seat. This gift is received only by faith. Nothing you can do. Your works don't count. You can't buy your way.

The ultimate example of God's release or remission is in His Son. Jesus forgives us of our debt, sin.

John 1:29 The next day he saw Jesus coming to him and said, "Behold, the Lamb of God who takes away the sin of the world!

Romans 5:9 Much more then, having now been justified by His blood, we shall be saved from the wrath *of God* through Him.

Believers in Christ are cleansed of sin by the innocent blood of the Lamb.

1 Peter 2:24 and He Himself bore our sins in His body on the cross, so that we might die to sin and live to righteousness; for by His wounds you were healed. Peter is quoting **Isaiah 53.**

Isaiah 53:5 But He was pierced through for our transgressions, He was crushed for our iniquities; the chastening for our well-being *fell* upon Him, and by His scourging we are healed.

Jesus Christ's work on the cross is our purification for sin. Jesus is the sacrificial paschal lamb. Christ's crown of thorns is the brushed blood on the lintel of the door. He is the shed blood on the doorposts with His outstretched arms on the cross.

John 1:29 Behold, the Lamb of God who takes away the sin of the world!

God saves us from sin via the shed blood of His Son. The fine has been paid. There are no strings or conditions attached. Our transgressions are forgiven as a matter of grace and mercy. Eternal life is a merciful, gracious gift, plain and simple.

Ephesians 1:7 In Him we have redemption through His blood, the forgiveness of our trespasses, according to the riches of His grace.

Christ's blood is the fulfillment of the propitiation or substitution. It is better than bleach. His shed blood satisfies the just nature of God. This is the only appeasement. There has to be a payment for all sin. Only the blood of Christ can wash away humanity's dross and impurities. Christ's shed blood is more powerful and cleanses better than fire. He is the one who purifies and refines. He removes the scum and the dregs.

1 John 1:7b …and the blood of Jesus His Son cleanses us from all sin.

Romans 3:25 whom God put forward as a propitiation by his blood, to be received by faith. This was to show God's righteousness, because in his divine forbearance he had passed over former sins.

1 John 2:2 and He Himself is the propitiation for our sins; and not for ours only, but also for *those of* the whole world.

Jesus forgives all sins. There is not a list of special exemptions or conditions.

1 John 1:7 But if we walk in the light, as he is in the light, we have fellowship with one another, and the blood of Jesus his Son cleanses us from <u>all</u> sin.

The Greek word for "all" used by John is πασ/pas. Per Strong's Concordance it means: each, every, any, all, the whole, everyone, all things, everything. ALL sin is forgiven.

With Jesus, forgiveness of sin is not a one-time special offer. "For this year only…" No, you can come to Jesus any time you want. Now would be a good time. It does not have to be a special year or date. When Jesus dealt with sin, it was taken care of once and for all time. All people are covered if they are accepting of His effort and payment.

1 Peter 3:18 For Christ also died for sins <u>once</u> for all, *the* just for *the* unjust, so that He might bring us to God, having been put to death in the flesh, but made alive in the spirit.

Romans 6:10a For the death that He died, He died to sin <u>once</u> for all…

Hebrews 9:28 so Christ, having been offered <u>once</u> to bear the sins of many, will appear a second time, not to deal with sin but to save those who are eagerly waiting for him.

Hebrews 10:10 And by that will, we have been sanctified through the sacrifice of the body of Jesus Christ <u>once for all</u>.

The Greek word for "once" is **ηαπαξ/hapax**. It means: once, one time, once for all. Christ's one and only death is enough to cover the sins of the planet across the ages.

So what if Jesus was not raised from the dead? What's the big deal about the resurrection? Who cares? Scripture states twice in the below verses, we are wasting our time with Christianity and the Bible if the resurrection is not true. Without the resurrection, we physically die and our bodies are eternally buried. Death wins. We are dirt and worm food. Our bodies become the byproduct of worm digestion...

Job 21:26 Together they lie down in the dust, and worms cover them.

Without Jesus' resurrection, our faith is described as **"vain"** and **"worthless"**.

1 Corinthians 15:14b <u>...your faith is also in vain.</u>

1 Corinthians 15:17 and if Christ has not been raised, <u>your faith is worthless</u>; you are still in your sins.

The Greek word for "vain" is **κενοσ/kenos.** It means: empty, devoid of truth; contains nothing; empty handed; without a gift; fruitless; no purpose.

The Greek word for "worthless" is **ματαιοσ/mataios.** It means: devoid of force, truth, success, result; useless, of no purpose. - Definitions per Strong's Concordance

This is our faith without the resurrection of Christ. Without Jesus' resurrection, there is no hope for our bodies. We are dead and buried, a corrupt and purposeless mess, an empty shell.

If we are not resurrected in the future, then Christ's resurrection in the past did not occur. We have historical proof of Jesus overcoming death with hundreds of witnesses. We know what happened to Jesus. This observation is stated at least twice by Paul. That's the security and truth of our future resurrection.

1 Corinthians 15:13 But if there is no resurrection of the dead, not even Christ has been raised...

1 Corinthians 15:16 For if the dead are not raised, not even Christ has been raised;

With the resurrection of Christ, **Psalm 16:10** was prophetically fulfilled.

Psalm 16:10 For You will not abandon my soul to Sheol; nor will You allow Your Holy One to undergo decay.

With His death, Jesus did not stay in Sheol or Hades or the grave (see **Ephesians 8-10**). There was no decomposition of His body.

Acts 2:31 Foreseeing this, David spoke about the resurrection of the Christ, that He was not abandoned to Hades, nor did His body see decay.

There are two words used for the concept of "resurrection". Here is how the words can be translated from the original Greek. The first example is in the verse below.

1 Corinthians 15:13 But if there is no <u>resurrection</u> of the dead, not even Christ has been raised;

The Greek word for "resurrection" is **αναστασισ/anastasis**. It means: raising up, rising (e.g. from a seat); a rising from the dead; that of Christ; that of all men at the end of this present age. -Strong's Concordance

The second example is "raised".

1 Corinthians 15:4 and that He was buried, and that He was <u>raised</u> on the third day according to the Scriptures...

The Greek word for "raised" is εγειρο/egeiro". It means: to awake, to arouse from the sleep of death, to recall the dead to life. -Strong's Concordance

The resurrection of Jesus is the power of God. The resurrection validates and authenticates Christ's death on the cross which is the payment for sin. The resurrection is dominance over death. It proved Jesus was deity. Jesus was literally raised out of, from among the dead. He is the first of the resurrection. Without the Jesus' resurrection, there is no hope for our bodies. He is the guarantee our resurrection. Without it, our faith is pointless. The promise of the resurrection is the reconnection of our body, soul, and spirit into a glorified body.

God the Father will judge the world through His Son Jesus. Based on what, the fact of the resurrection.

Acts 17:31 because He has fixed a day in which He will judge the world in righteousness through a Man whom He has appointed, having furnished proof to all men by raising Him from the dead."

Currently, Jesus is our High Priest in Heaven. He is our representative before the Father. At this time, we do not need an earthly priest. The Pope, a priest, or any other human agent on earth does not represent us before God the Father. The individual believer has direct access to God the Father via God the Son because we are sealed with God the Spirit.

Hebrews 7:24-26 but Jesus, on the other hand, because He continues forever, holds His priesthood permanently. Therefore He is able also to save forever those who draw near to God through Him, since He always lives to make intercession for them. For it was fitting for us to have such a high priest, holy, innocent, undefiled, separated from sinners and exalted above the heavens.

The gospel is not a New Testament phenomenon as some critics would have us believe. How many times have we heard, "The God of the Old Testament is a mean, cruel killer!" God is not an oppressive ogre who wants to crush you with His thumb. He has always been merciful, gracious, and forgiving. Honestly, if God smashed us like a bug any time we screwed up…would there be any humanity left? The good news has always been there. His redemption for humanity was promised from the beginning of time in the Garden of Eden. God delivered the "good news" to Satan.

Genesis 3:15 And I will put enmity between you and the woman, and between your seed and her seed; He shall bruise you on the head, and you shall bruise him on the heel.

Just in case anyone is wondering, the message of a sacrificial death for sin rings loud and clear in the Old Testament. The best example of the gospel in the Old Testament comes from the Prophet **Isaiah** about 700 years before Jesus Christ walked the earth. Look at the detail of these verses. It reads as a narrative of the events along with the accounts in **Matthew, Mark, Luke,** and **John**.

Isaiah 53:3-12 He was despised and forsaken of men, a man of sorrows and acquainted with grief; and like one from whom men hide their face He was despised, and we did not esteem Him. Surely our griefs He Himself bore, and our sorrows He carried; yet we ourselves esteemed Him stricken, smitten of God, and afflicted. But He was pierced through for our transgressions, He was crushed for our iniquities; the chastening for our well-being *fell* upon Him, and by His scourging we are healed. All of us like sheep have gone astray, each of us has turned to his own way; but the LORD has caused the iniquity of us all to fall on Him. He was oppressed and He was afflicted, yet He did not open His mouth; like a lamb that is led to slaughter, and like a sheep that is silent before its shearers, so He did not open His mouth. By oppression and judgment He was taken away; and as for His generation, who considered that He was cut off out of the land of the living for the transgression of my people, to whom the stroke *was due?* His grave was assigned with wicked men, yet He was with a rich man in His death, because He had done no violence, nor was there any deceit in His mouth. But the LORD was pleased to crush Him, putting *Him* to grief; if He would render Himself *as* a guilt offering, He will see *His* offspring, He will

prolong *His* days, and the good pleasure of the LORD will prosper in His hand. As a result of the anguish of His soul, He will see *it and* be satisfied; by His knowledge the Righteous One, My Servant, will justify the many, as He will bear their iniquities. Therefore, I will allot Him a portion with the great, and He will divide the booty with the strong; because He poured out Himself to death, and was numbered with the transgressors; yet He Himself bore the sin of many, and interceded for the transgressors.

This book the Bible, says His Son, Jesus Christ, is physically coming back in the clouds to get His people the church, at the resurrection and the rapture. Then, He will return later to establish His kingdom on earth.

And that is good news. Jesus is the Messiah, just believe it.

John 20:31 But these are written so that you may *believe* Jesus is the Messiah, the Son of God, and by *believing* you may have life in His name.

Hebrews 11:6 And without *faith* it is impossible to please *Him,* for he who comes to God *must believe* that He is and *that* He is a rewarder of those who seek Him.

Chapter 3
Well That's Your Interpretation

How does one view the Bible? Is it a book of stories? Are the stories true? Or are they fables with a moral? Are these real people in the Bible? Does God really mean that?

The Bible is a book of many components and categories. There is history, law, poetry, song, morality, and prophecy.

There are figures of speech and idiomatic language. Metaphorical language is not the same from language to language and culture to culture. There are differences from generation to generation. Sometimes there is confusion determining meaning if the context and use of language is literal or idiomatic. Is that a figure of speech or not? Believe me that will matter when we dive into this topic.

Context matters and Scripture needs to be understood within its context. How I write professionally as a healthcare provider is not the same as how I write a book or how I write an email. The context matters and changes.

Words mean things…consistently. Can you imagine trying to have a conversation if words changed meaning? "Well, that word has about five meanings to me." It would be impossible and crazy to communicate. "What did you really *mean* with that statement?"

Once upon a time, humanity spoke one language. People apparently were pretty good with communication in the past. Clearly it is effective to use the same words with consistent meaning. So good, humanity needed to have their language scrambled. For those who like to allegorize, Scripture and God make an excellent case against your view of interpretation.

Genesis 11:1 Now the whole earth used the same language and the same words.

Consistent semantics and syntax are a good thing when channeled in the right direction.

Genesis 11:6 The LORD said, "Behold, they are one people, and they all have the same language. And this is what they began to do, and now nothing which they purpose to do will be impossible for them.

But when language was abused and humanity was disobedient, God took action.

Genesis 11:9 Therefore its name was called Babel, because there the LORD confused the language of the whole earth; and from there the LORD scattered them abroad over the face of the whole earth.

Because of God's action, it is important to look at the original languages of the Bible and how they function. The Old Testament was written primarily in Hebrew with a few exceptions of Aramaic. The New Testament was written in common Greek. Culturally, east meets west with these two languages. Sometimes there are not perfect translations. Mindsets, philosophies, and civilizations clash. This book is being written by a man living in 21st century America. My world is a completely different world.

Time, place, and circumstances are factors. Think of communication today. Do today's youth talk and communicate with each other like their parents? Hardly. We used to talk when we were kids. Millennials sit around a couch and text each other. Millennials use short hand code and emojis. We could spell words and use sentences and talk.

There will be one universal language in the Millennial Kingdom. The same language and the same words will be used again by all. **Zephaniah 3:9** will undo the scattering and confusion created at Babel. In the Millennial Kingdom, humanity will be under the leadership of Jesus. People will be personally taught by Him in His ways. Under the leadership of Christ, people should generally have a better sense of direction and focus.

Zephaniah 3:9 For then I will give to the peoples purified lips, that all of them may call on the name of the LORD, To serve Him shoulder to shoulder.

What in the world are **purified lips**? The Hebrew word for "lips" is **saphah.** Per Strong's Concordance it means: lip, language, speech. The term "lip" is synonymous with a language or speech.

The New Testament equivalent is "tongue" or **glossa** in the Greek.

For example **Acts 2:4 And they were all filled with the Holy Spirit and began to speak with other tongues, as the Spirit was giving them utterance.**

The Bible is talking about foreign languages. This is not a reference to a bunch of "spiritual" non-intelligible mumbo jumbo that nobody knows what is being said.

1 Corinthians 14:4 The one who speaks in a tongue builds up himself, but the one who prophesies builds up the church. Get over yourself. If nobody understands it, what good is it? The context of **1 Corinthians 14** is a discussion about foreign languages. There are better gifts, desire those.

The future kingdom holds one language.

"Purified"…The Hebrew word is **barar**. It means: to purge out, purify, to choose, select; to cleanse, make shining, polish. It is a simple action verb in Hebrew.

The context of the verse in **Zephaniah 3** is all the **peoples. Verse 6** mentions **"nations". Verse 8** talks about the **"nations, kingdoms and the whole earth". Verse 19** states the **"whole earth". Verse 20** discusses the **"nations of the earth".**

Simply stated, God is going to purge the languages and choose one. **Zephaniah 3:9** states there will be one language spoken on Earth in the Millennial Kingdom. I suspect the chosen language will be Hebrew, but whatever God chooses.

But we are not in the Millennial Kingdom just yet. So the New Testament was written roughly 2,000 years ago. The Old Testament was written across 2,400 to 3,600 years ago. The point is, communication styles change. We need to try and place ourselves in the past and understand their ways.

In the beginning…

Creation was spoke into existence with a word in **Genesis**. God and the Word are synonymous.

John 1:1-2 In the beginning was the Word, and the Word was with God, and the Word was God. He was in the beginning with God.

The above verses are not up for debate. It is either true or false. Where do you stand? Make a decision.

2 Timothy 3:16-17 <u>All Scripture</u> is inspired by God and profitable for teaching, for reproof, for correction, for training in righteousness; so that the man of God may be adequate, equipped for every good work.

This word given to us is more sure than what our senses detect. The Word is better than what we can feel, touch, taste, smell, or hear.

2 Peter 1:19 And we have the <u>more certain</u> prophetic word, to which you do well taking heed, as to a lamp shining in a dark place, until this day shall have dawned and *the* morning star shall have arisen in your hearts...

Culturally Jewish

The Bible is a culturally Jewish book. God defined what it is to be a Hebrew. He created the country of Israel through the person of Jacob. The nation Israel would come from this man. In the original Hebrew language per Strong's Concordance, Jacob means "heel holder" or "supplanter". It can also mean he cheats or deceives. Jacob was given this name because of the events at his birth.

Genesis 25:26a Afterward his brother came forth with his hand holding on to Esau's heel, so his name was called Jacob...

This name accurately describes Jacob. He cheated and deceived his brother Esau for his inheritance. The deceiver met his match in his future father in law, Laban (**Genesis 29-31**).

Genesis 32:28 Then he said, "Your name shall no longer be called Jacob, but Israel, for you have striven with God and with men, and have prevailed."

God changed Jacob's name to Israel. In the Hebrew (Strong's Concordance), Israel means "God prevails". Per Holman's Bible Dictionary, Israel means: God strives, God rules, God heals, or he strives against God.

Jesus is a Jew. He was born a Jew. He was raised in Jewish home with Jewish parents Joseph and Mary. He lived in Israel, a Hebrew nation. We worship a Jewish carpenter.

Matthew, the author of the self-named gospel is a Jew. Mark, another gospel author is a Jew.

Paul the Super Jew

The ultimate example of a Jew's Jew is the Apostle Paul. The Apostle Paul (name means short) is the author of 13 letters in the New Testament. Scholars argue that he is possibly the author of Hebrews as well.

Paul was born as Saul in the city of Tarsus in the region of Cilicia. Tarsus is located near the northeastern corner of the Mediterranean Sea. He grew up in Jerusalem and studied under the famous teacher Gamaliel.

Acts 22:3 "I am a Jew, born in Tarsus of Cilicia, but brought up in this city, educated under Gamaliel, strictly according to the law of our fathers, being zealous for God just as you all are today."

Paul's father was a member of the Pharisees. The apostle was raised a Jew. The context of the verse below is an argument between two groups of Jews, Pharisees and Sadducees. Pharisees believed in the resurrection and rapture. The Sadducees did not. This was the Jewish religious version of Catholics and Protestants.

Acts 23:6 But perceiving that one group were Sadducees and the other Pharisees, Paul *began* crying out in the Council, "Brethren, I am a Pharisee, a son of Pharisees; I am on trial for the hope and resurrection of the dead!"

Paul was on trial for believing in "**hope**", the blessed hope of the rapture. Notice "hope" and "resurrection" in **Acts 23:6** are different and separated terms.

Titus 2:13 ...looking for the blessed hope and the appearing of the glory of our great God and Savior, Christ Jesus...

He was born a Jew of the tribe of Benjamin and he was a member of the Pharisees. Prior to his conversion, Saul was not a friend of believers in Jesus. He arrested and imprisoned believers. He was extremely zealous and had passion for Judaism. He was a Hebrew of Hebrews. He chased, persecuted, and blasphemed Christians to distant cities.

Philippians 3:5-6 circumcised the eighth day, of the nation of Israel, of the tribe of Benjamin, a Hebrew of Hebrews; as to the Law, a Pharisee; as to zeal, a persecutor of the church; as to the righteousness which is in the Law, found blameless.

Approval of death and persecution of believers was given by Paul. He was present at the stoning of the martyr Stephen.

Acts 7:58 When they had driven him out of the city, they *began* stoning *him;* and the witnesses laid aside their robes at the feet of a young man named Saul.

Paul was complicit in the stoning of Stephen. In return, he was stoned himself.

Acts 14:19 But Jews came from Antioch and Iconium, and having won over the crowds, they stoned Paul and dragged him out of the city, supposing him to be dead.

Stoning was a death sentence for a severe crime in the Mosaic Law. Stoning involved the entire community. The community assisted and participated in the stoning of an individual. The Jewish community had determined Paul the Jew needed to go.

Deuteronomy 21:21 Then all the men of his city shall stone him to death; so you shall remove the evil from your midst, and all Israel will hear *of it* and fear.

2 Corinthians 11:24 Five times I received from the Jews thirty-nine *lashes*.

Stoning and lashings were punishments for crimes committed per the Mosaic Law. Forty lashings were the standard amount of lashings per Jewish Law. To make sure they themselves did not break the law, administrators of punishment only gave 39 just in case they miscounted.

Deuteronomy 25:3 He may beat him forty times *but* no more, so that he does not beat him with many more stripes than these and your brother is not degraded in your eyes.

Paul even described his own behavior as exceedingly mad or furious. He was a passionate Jew. Paul was committed to the cause of Judaism. He was a ring leader. The legalist loved enforcing the law. He tried to manipulate non-Jews into punishable crimes. Paul the Jew chased Christians all over the Middle East and Turkey.

Acts 26:10-11 And this is just what I did in Jerusalem; not only did I lock up many of the saints in prisons, having received authority from the chief priests, but also when they were being put to death I cast my vote against them. And as I punished them often in all the synagogues, I tried to force them to blaspheme; and being furiously enraged at them, I kept pursuing them even to foreign cities.

Paul by trade was a tentmaker. Tents were primarily made of goat hair back in the day. An extra Biblical source (Holman Bible Dictionary) indicates that Paul's family was moderately wealthy deriving their income from leather goods and tent making.

Acts 18:3 and because he was of the same trade, he stayed with them and they were working, for by trade they were tent-makers.

In retrospect the Apostle Paul was humbled by the Lord Jesus Christ Himself, a Jew.

Culturally, the Bible is a Jewish book in the Middle East. In general, the Bible was written by Jewish men. It is not to be viewed from a western culture perspective. To properly understand the Bible, we need to go back in time 2,000 plus years and try to understand Hebrew culture. We are missing out on a greater understanding and limiting ourselves if we choose not to look at the writings in their cultural context.

Chapter 4
Relative to What?

When does the rapture occur? Some believe there is no such doctrine called the rapture in the Bible. One has to admit. The idea of people lifting off of the planet into the clouds is pretty fantastic. Believers in Jesus will essentially disappear into thin air. There are many perspectives in regards to the time when the rapture of the church occurs relative to the great tribulation, the wrath of God.

Imminence

The first line of thought discussed is the rapture is imminent and before the tribulation. It could happen at any time. The rapture will come without warning. It will be sudden. Mark Hitchcock has stated the rapture is a signless event. The rapture is not dependent on any other Biblical event to take place before it occurs. Believers in Christ are raptured to Heaven and return to Earth at least seven years or more later (The Four Horsemen of the Apocalypse, p.14). Imminent rapture theorists believe one can know the season of the Lord's return for His bride the church. But we are unable to know the exact date in light of **Matthew 24:44**. The verse states, **"For this reason you also must be ready; for the Son of Man is coming at an hour when you do not think *He will.*"** -Jesus

Matthew 25:13 "Be on the alert then, for you do not know the day nor the hour." -Jesus

The context of the verse above is Jesus discussing the signs regarding the end of the age and His return to Earth.

Supporters of an imminent rapture position take a literal meaning to the verses in **Matthew 24:44** and **Matthew 25:13**. This author thinks there is a language, cultural and custom barrier to our 21st century Western minds. Personally, I do not take these verses literally. I believe the language is idiomatic in a Hebraic mindset. Please hold those thoughts and questions. An explanation is coming later.

A list of imminent rapture scholars, teacher, authors, and thinkers include the late Tim LaHaye of the Left Behind book series, Mark Hitchcock, Dan Goodwin, and Thomas Ice among many others.

The reply to this imminent rapture position lies in the resurrection of the dead in Jesus Christ. The dead in Christ will rise first and ascend into Heaven before the rapture occurs. Yes, there is a historical event that will preceded the rapture. It is the resurrection. See the following examples from Scripture below.

A great detailed explanation of these events is **1 Corinthians 15** written by the Apostle Paul. Specifically look at **1 Corinthians 15:51-52 Behold, I tell you a mystery; we will not all sleep, but we will all be changed, in a moment, in the twinkling of an eye, at the last trumpet; for the trumpet will sound, and the dead will be raised imperishable, and we will be changed.**

The idea of sleep communicated by the Apostle Paul is physical death. When we die, our body is buried and sleeping in the ground like a seed as stated earlier in **1 Corinthians 15:42-44**. Sleep implies the body will wake up at some point in the future. The new information conveyed is **we will not all sleep.** Translation, believers will not all physically die. The sequence of events is described next. One, **the dead will be raised imperishable** (resurrection)**.** Two, believers in Jesus who are alive and remaining…**we will be changed** (rapture).

The order of events is confirmed a second time in **1 Thessalonians 4:15-17**. The resurrection happens **first. Then** the rapture occurs second. Dead believers go first.

1 Thessalonians 4:15-17 For this we say to you by the word of the Lord, that we who are alive and remain until the coming of the Lord, will not precede those who have fallen asleep. For the Lord Himself will descend from heaven with a shout, with the voice of the archangel and with the trumpet of God, and the dead in Christ will rise first. Then we who are alive and remain will be caught up together with them in the clouds to meet the Lord in the air, and so we shall always be with the Lord.

The time frame between the resurrection and rapture is not stated. There is no time marker. It could be seven seconds or seven years.

The text does not say. But, the resurrection of the dead in Christ does come first. I suppose the timing of the two events would be relative to "imminent".

When the inhabitants of planet earth see thousands upon thousands of people arise from their graves and rise into the air, this will cause a variety of responses which will likely include chaos and confusion. This is not the Zombie Apocalypse the culture is expecting. Living believers should know their ascent into the clouds to join the resurrected and Jesus Christ is next in the order of events.

Pre Tribulation Rapture

Simply stated, a pre tribulation rapture position believes the entire body of the church of Jesus Christ will be caught up into the clouds to meet Him in the air. The resurrected believers will go first then those who are alive and remaining will go up next. This event will occur before the beginning of the seven year hell on earth that is the Tribulation or the Day of the Lord.

1 Thessalonians 4:16-17 For the Lord Himself will descend from heaven with a shout, with the voice of *the* archangel and with the trumpet of God, and the dead in Christ will rise first. Then we who are alive and remain will be caught up together with them in the clouds to meet the Lord in the air, and so we shall always be with the Lord.

This is the position of the author of this book. I believe in a pre-tribulation rapture. The book is an apologetic of the concept, no apologies. That said, I am not the only person who believes this.

Many scholars and authors hold to this position. This is a distinguished short list of many. Other pre tribulation experts include: Dr. Thomas Ice, the executive director of the Pre Trib Research Center, author Tim LaHaye of the best-selling Left Behind Book series, Dr. John Walvoord former President of Dallas Theological Seminary, and Professor J. Dwight Pentecost, Th. D. and author of Things to Come, A Study in Biblical Eschatology.

Who is John Nelson Darby?

John Darby was born in Westminster, London, England. He was an Anglo-Irish Bible teacher. He was a co-founder of the Plymouth Brethren. John was a leader in the Church of Ireland. Darby is considered the father of the pre tribulation rapture movement. His pre tribulation teachings gained traction during the 1830's. Darby's theological ideas reached the United States and spread via the Scofield Reference Bible in the early 20th century. Does this man have his critics!

Many critics of the pre tribulation position are absolutely convinced this doctrine did not exist prior to John Nelson Darby. Frankly, I did not want to discuss Darby at the outset of writing this book. This man is a clear stumbling block for many in their view of the end time's scenario. They can't get past Darby to research the evidence or read the Scriptural text.

There are all kinds of conspiracy theories attached to Darby. He was a tool against the Jesuits and the Catholic Church. He made up the position to combat any tribulation rapture view. Darby came along to counter the Reformation. He was called a heretic of the gospel of Jesus Christ by his contemporaries. I could go on and on and on. Darby has become the boogie man for the pre tribulation rapture position. The point is not to defend Darby. There has been enough written about and against John Nelson Darby. Let the man rest in peace.

https://en.wikipedia.org/wiki/John_Nelson_Darby

What I will discuss is the notion of the genesis of the pre tribulation rapture position. There are multiple examples of scholars and early church leaders way before Darby who were pre tribulation in their rapture thinking. I was able to find four people prior to Darby in the 1830's who were pre tribulation believers. Excerpts provided by Dan Goodwin, God's Final Jubilee, p. 11-12, 2014, Goodwin Publications.

Joseph Mede, "I will add this more, namely, what may be conceived to be the cause of the RAPTURE of the saints on high to meet the Lord in the clouds, rather than to wait his coming to earth…What if it be, that they may be PRESERVED during the Conflagration of the earth and the works thereof, **2 Peter 3:10**, that as Noah and his family were preserved from the Deluge by being lift up above the waters in the Ark; so should the saints at the Conflagration be lift up in the clouds unto their Ark, Christ to be preserved there from the deluge of fire, wherein the wicked shall be consumed?"

The Works of Joseph Mede, 1672 AD, London Edition, Book IV, p. 776.

For all the saints and elect of God are gathered, prior to the tribulation that is to come, and are taken to the Lord lest they see the confusion that is to overwhelm the world because of our sins.

Ephraim the Syrian, "On the Last Times 2", 306 AD - 373 AD.

"We that see that terrible things have begun, and know that still more terrible things are imminent, may regard it as the greatest advantage to depart from it as quickly as possible. Do you not give God thanks, do you not congratulate yourself, that by an early departure you are taken away, and delivered from the shipwrecks and disasters that are imminent?"

"Treatise of Cyprian", 200 AD - 258 AD.

"And therefore, when in the end the Church shall be suddenly caught up from this, it is said, 'There shall be tribulation such as has not been since the beginning, neither shall be.' For this is the last contest of the righteous, in which, when they overcome they are crowned with incorruption."

Irenaeus, "Against Heresies", 130 AD - 202 AD.

Irenaeus was an eyewitness to the Apostle John and a disciple of Polycarp. Polycarp served as the minister of Smyrna. This is the same Polycarp who was martyred in the Revelation church of Smyrna (See **Revelation 2:8-11**). One can find Polycarp's grave in modern day Izmir, Turkey. Irenaeus received his information from the man and Apostle John, who was tight with Jesus. I would consider Irenaeus to be very reliable source.

I would argue the Apostle Paul was the first pre-tribulation scholar. He informed the Thessalonians from the outset of his letter, Jesus will deliver believers. You are not appointed to judgment or wrath.

1 Thessalonians 1:10 and to wait for His Son from heaven, whom He raised from the dead, *that is* Jesus, who rescues us from the wrath to come.

The Greek word **οργε/orge** is translated as "wrath" in English. Believers are spared God's **orge** or wrath. -Strong's Concordance

This is the context of **1 Thessalonians**. Some rebel rouser was stirring up trouble in the local body or church in Thessalonica. He was falsely teaching the resurrection and the rapture had already come. Believers were freaking out they had missed the blessed hope of Jesus gathering up His bride, the church.

1 Thessalonians 4:13 But we do not want you to be uninformed, brethren, about those who are asleep, so that you will not grieve as do the rest who have no hope.

The members of the church had been previously informed. They had been taught. They needed reminding. Paul spends the next few verses in **1 Thessalonians 5** reminding them of their position. You guys know! You are enlightened!

There is a difference and a contrast to the church "in the know" and for those claiming **"Peace and safety!"** Watch out. There is no escape or deliverance for the peaceniks. Man's proclamation of peace is hollow and results in sudden death.

1 Thessalonians 5:1-5 Now as to the times and the epochs, brethren, you have no need of anything to be written to you. For you yourselves know full well that the day of the Lord will come just like a thief in the night. While they are saying, "Peace and safety!" then destruction will come upon them suddenly like labor pains upon a woman with child, and they will not escape. But you, brethren, are not in darkness, that the day would overtake you like a thief; for you are all sons of light and sons of day. We are not of night nor of darkness...

Again, Paul reminds them. You are not going to experience God's judgment but you will receive His safety and deliverance.

1 Thessalonians 5:9 For God has not destined us for wrath, but for obtaining salvation through our Lord Jesus Christ...

The point of the letter to the Thessalonians was to provide comfort and encouragement. The resurrection and the rapture have not happened. It is going to be just fine.

1 Thessalonians 4:18 Therefore comfort one another with these words.

1 Thessalonians 5:11 Therefore encourage one another and build up one another, just as you also are doing.

We would all do well to follow the advice of Paul in **1 Thessalonians 5:21 But examine everything carefully; hold fast to that which is good...**

All of that said, John Nelson Darby was NOT the first pre tribulation rapture theorist, end of discussion.

Mid Tribulation

A third theory is called the Mid Tribulation Rapture (rapture in the middle). Proponents of this theory believe the rapture occurs at the midway point of the seven year tribulation. That would be three and one half years from the signing of the peace treaty with Israel and Arabs. The antichrist will broker the peace deal. The lawless one will be on the scene. The church would know and see the antichrist.

Within the Mid Tribulation position are a couple of ideas in regards to the timing of the event. From a timing standpoint, what event is the halfway point? The other question, when does God's wrath officially begin?

That is a sticking point because the church is not appointed to wrath. How is wrath defined? The Greek word is **οργε/orge.** It is defined as: anger, indignation; anger exhibited in punishment, hence used for punishment itself; of punishments inflicted by magistrates. -Strong's Concordance

Orge is the Greek word used in **Romans 5:9, 1 Thessalonians 1:10** and **5:9.** It is translated as "wrath" in all three instances.

Below are three of several examples showing the church is spared from God's **orge** or wrath.

1 Thessalonians 1:10 and to wait for His Son from heaven, whom He raised from the dead, that is Jesus, who rescues us from the <u>wrath</u> to come.

Romans 5:9 Much more then, having now been justified by His blood, we shall be saved from the <u>wrath</u> *of God* through Him.

1 Thessalonians 5:9 For God has not destined us for <u>wrath</u>, but to obtain salvation through our Lord Jesus Christ…

There are two verses Mid Tribulation theorists point towards as possible halfway events in the seven year tribulation. The first verse is **Revelation 6:17…for the great day of their <u>wrath</u> has come, and who is able to stand?**

The Greek word for "wrath" in **Revelation 6:17** is οργε/orge. It is the same word the church is spared in **1 Thessalonians 1:10, Romans 5:9,** and **1 Thessalonians 5:9.**

The second possible halfway point verse is **Revelation 11:15.** This is the sounding of the seventh and last trumpet in **Revelation**. Some scholars think this is the reference for the last trump in **1 Corinthians 15:52 in a moment, in the twinkling of an eye, <u>at the last trumpet</u>; for the trumpet will sound, and the dead will be raised imperishable, and we will be changed.**

God's two witness have been murdered, resurrected, and ascended into Heaven. A massive earthquake has occurred culminating the sixth trumpet. The previous verse **Revelation 11:14** indicates two woes are over and the third one is coming. There is a clean break and pause in the judgment.

Revelation 11:14 The second woe is past; behold, the third woe is coming quickly.

The most straight forward argument against the Mid Tribulation rapture lies in the transition from **Revelation 3** to **Revelation 4.**

John received the message for **Revelation 1-3** on the island of Patmos in the Aegean Sea off the western coast of Turkey. Jesus has finished His message to the seven churches. Where were the churches located? The churches were in real historical cities. They were in seven cities in what is modern day western Turkey on planet Earth.

Starting in **Revelation 4**, John was called into Heaven. **Revelation 4:1 After these things I looked, and behold, a door standing open in <u>heaven</u>, and the first voice which I had heard, like the sound of a trumpet speaking with me, said, "<u>Come up here</u>, and I will show you what must take place after these things."**

John is in the throne room of Heaven as described in **Revelation 4:2-3.** He also has the company of elders with white garments and golden crowns. **Revelation 4:4 Around the throne were twenty-four thrones; and upon the thrones I saw twenty-four elders sitting, clothed in white garments, and golden crowns on their heads.**

This is a description of the church. Leadership in local churches are comprised of elders. Their garments have been washed clean in the blood of the Lamb. They have overcome and received a crown of gold. The white garments and the gold are the promises of Jesus Christ in His letters to the churches in **Revelation 3:4** and **3:18.**

Revelation 3:4 But you do have a few people in Sardis who have not soiled their <u>garments</u>, and because they are worthy, they will walk with Me in <u>white</u>.

Revelation 3:18 I counsel you to buy from Me <u>gold</u> refined by fire so that you may become rich, <u>white garments</u> so that you may be clothed and your shameful nakedness not exposed, and salve to anoint your eyes so that you may see.

In **Revelation 4**, the church is in Heaven and they have received their rewards. God's wrath and tribulation takes place on Earth. The body of Christ is safe and away from the planet in Heaven. Judgment on those remaining inhabitants of Earth has not yet started. Judgment does not start until **Revelation 6** and the four horsemen of the Apocalypse.

A second argument against a Mid Tribulation theory lies in **2 Thessalonians 2:3 Let no one deceive you in any way. For that day will not come, unless the rebellion comes first, and the man of lawlessness is revealed, the son of destruction…**

The "day" referenced is the Day of the Lord as noted in the previous verse. The Day of the Lord is a term synonymous with the great tribulation. God's wrath will not come until the man of lawlessness is revealed. The man of lawlessness is none other than the antichrist. There must be the antichrist before the world has seven years of God's judgment.

A few verses later in **2 Thessalonians 2**, the Apostle Paul further explains the antichrist is restrained. The verses below give the sequence of events: antichrist restrained, rapture, antichrist revealed, tribulation, second coming of Jesus Christ, and the end of the antichrist.

2 Thessalonians 2:6-8a And you know what <u>restrains</u> him now, so that in his time he will be revealed. For the mystery of lawlessness is already at work; only he who now <u>restrains</u> will do so until he is taken out of the way. Then that lawless one will be revealed whom the Lord will slay with the breath of His mouth and bring to an end by the appearance of His coming…

The lawless one will not be known to the world until the restrainer is removed. So who is the restrainer? It is the Holy Spirit. God the Spirit restrains the antichrist. The Spirit of God resides in the believers of the body of Jesus Christ. These verses state Spirit indwelled believers will be leaving before the antichrist is known and the great tribulation starts. We will be **taken out of the way. Then that lawless one will be revealed.**

Mid Tribulation theory has the church being on earth and seeing the antichrist. This is not possible per the verses in **2 Thessalonians 2**.

The third concept against a Mid Tribulation rapture event is expressed in **Revelation 7:14 I said to him, "My lord, you know." And he said to me, "These are the ones who come out of the great tribulation, and they have washed their robes and made them white in the blood of the Lamb.**

The context of the conversation is an elder who is talking to John. Remember, an elder is a member of the body of Christ or the church. The elder has been in the throne room of Heaven since **Revelation 4**. The elder has no clue who these people are in Heaven in **Revelation 7**. The time point is between the seal and trumpet judgments. Only the seals have been broken and completed. The trumpet judgments are yet to come.

People will die during the first six seal judgments. There will be millions of people left behind on Earth after the resurrection and rapture. I have no doubt some will have their literal come to Jesus moment sometime after the rapture and before the end of the sixth seal. I take it **these are the ones who come out of the great tribulation.** Notice, the first six seals are considered to be in the great tribulation per **Revelation 7:14.**

Mid Tribulation theorists have the rapture occurring at this time point after the sixth seal in **Revelation 6:17** or later in **Revelation 11.** In either case, Scripture states in **Revelation 7:14** the events preceding these points in time are considered part of the **great tribulation.**

Post Tribulation

Another theory is a Post Tribulation Rapture (rapture after). Believers in this theory indicate the church will go through the great tribulation. The body of Christ will remain on Earth during the seven years of judgment. Post tribulation states the church will see and experience the wrath of the antichrist. They also think the resurrection and the rapture will occur at the end of the tribulation. Then they will immediately descend back to the earth with Jesus at His second advent.

Post tribulation theorists teach the idea of a pre tribulation rapture started with John Darby in Great Britain. See the previous discussion on Darby in the pre tribulation section. They also think pre tribulation rapture grabbed hold in the United States with the Scofield Reference Bible. Post tribulation thinkers state their position is that of the early church.

From their standpoint, the timing of the rapture is knowable. It is seven years after the start of the tribulation, so much for an imminent rapture.

Post tribbers think the church is promised tribulation. An example is listed below.

Matthew 24:9-11 "Then they will deliver you to tribulation, and will kill you, and you will be hated by all nations because of My name. At that time many will fall away and will betray one another and hate one another. Many false prophets will arise and will mislead many…"

These verses in **Matthew** are addressing Israel, not the church. Tribulation is promised to Israel, not the church. The problem lies in confusion between the church and Israel, two distinct groups. This concept will be discussed at length later in the book.

Partial

Another position is the Partial Rapture theory. With the Partial Rapture, a remnant of believers will be left behind. They will be left to endure the seven year tribulation and judgment. All believers will not be raptured when the time comes. The thinking is only the faithful and watchful believers in Jesus will be snatched into the clouds by the Lord.

I guess these folks of the Partial Rapture theory posit that only the Spiritual Elite will make into the clouds. The issue against this line of thinking would be the death of Jesus Christ. He died for all sin, once and for all. Below are three verses of many that communicate this concept.

1 Peter 3:18 For Christ also died for sins <u>once for all</u>, the just for the unjust, so that He might bring us to God, having been put to death in the flesh, but made alive in the spirit…

Romans 6:10 For the death that He died, He died to sin <u>once for</u> <u>all</u>; but the life that He lives, He lives to God.

Hebrews 9:28 so Christ also, having been offered <u>once</u> to bear the sins of many, will appear a second time for salvation without reference to sin, to those who eagerly await Him.

The phrase "once for all" in English is the Greek word ηαπαξ/**hapax.** Per Strong's Concordance **hapax** is defined as once, once for all.

Jesus died for the sins of the entire world including those who refuse (their problem not His). We are talking about a set of people who believe Jesus died for their sin. Partial rapture theory says Jesus will turn His back on a set of believers who believe He died for their sins. Did Jesus do enough at the cross for sin? Was sin paid for or not? I don't see Jesus turning His back on a portion of His body.

Besides, His body the church is a living, breathing organism that is one body.

Ephesians 5:29-30 for no one ever hated his own flesh, but nourishes and cherishes it, just as Christ also does the church, because we are members of His body.

Jesus is taking His entire body. Christ does not hate believers. The text says He nourishes and cherishes His church. The verb tense in the original Greek indicates the action by Jesus Christ is continual and all the time. Jesus will continually feed and nourish His church. Christ will continually love, warm, and foster His body with tenderness.

The passages in **1 Corinthians 15:51-52** make it very clear…all…The Greek word is πασ/**pas.** It can be translated as: all, any, every, the whole. -Strong's Concordance

1 Corinthians 15:51-52 Behold, I tell you a mystery; we will not <u>all</u> sleep, but we will <u>all</u> be changed, in a moment, in the twinkling of an eye, at the last trumpet; for the trumpet will sound, and the dead will be raised imperishable, and we will be changed.

He paid for **ALL** of those who believe He died for sin at the cross. It is redemption time.

Pan Rapture

The last is the Pan Rapture position. These folks are not concerned about the timing of the rapture. God the Father, the Son, and the Spirit are in control and it is all going to "pan" out. Don't worry, be happy.

What if Noah had this "pan rapture" attitude in **Genesis**?

Genesis 6:13-14 Then God said to Noah, "The end of all flesh has come before Me; for the earth is filled with violence because of them; and behold, I am about to destroy them with the earth. Make for yourself an ark of gopher wood; you shall make the ark with rooms, and shall cover it inside and out with pitch."

Genesis 6:17 "Behold, I, even I am bringing the flood of water upon the earth, to destroy all flesh in which is the breath of life, from under heaven; everything that is on the earth shall perish."

What if Noah decided not to act on this information? Noah could have believed God but chose to do nothing. We are not here if Noah had not followed God's directions.

Genesis 6:22 Thus Noah did; according to all that God had commanded him, so he did.

Thank God for directions and thank Noah for obedience.

The Tribulation is a seven year period of Divine judgment on the people of planet earth because of our sin. It is a matter of simple justice. Approximately 13% of the Bible is written about this seven year period. If the data points of time in the Bible are taken literally in terms of ages of people and reigns of leaders, the earth is roughly 6,000 years old. This seven year period represents .0012 of history (7/6000). Approximately 13% of the Bible focuses on .12% of history! Two chapters in **Genesis** were dedicated to Noah's flood. Humanity is being given disproportionate, ample, and considerable warning. If we are given information, then we are called to action.

We need to get our personal spiritual house in order before the great and terrible Day of the Lord!

Jesus held the religious leaders of His day accountable to know His arrival was here. The Bible foretold in prophecy the arrival of the Messiah and His character and deeds. Of all the people who should have known, it was the religious leaders of the Temple.

Matthew 16:1-3 And having come the Pharisees and Sadducees tempting, asked Him to show them a sign out of the heaven. But answering, He said to them, Evening coming on, you say, Clear sky, for the sky is red. And at morning, today a storm, for the sky is red, being overcast. Hypocrites! You indeed know how to discern the face of the heaven, but you cannot the signs of the times. -Jesus

The city of Jerusalem was held accountable for not accepting Jesus Christ as their Messiah at His first advent. Their rejection of Christ continues to have consequences to this day in the 21st century. They should have known He was coming. His character was on display for His three and a half year ministry.

Luke 13:34-35 "O Jerusalem, Jerusalem, the city that kills the prophets and stones those sent to her! How often I wanted to gather your children together, just as a hen gathers her brood under her wings, and you would not have it! Behold, your house is left to you desolate; and I say to you, you will not see Me until the time comes when you say, 'Blessed is he who comes in the name of the Lord!'"

Jesus is quoting **Psalm 118:26** in the last portion of **Luke 13:35.**

The same is true for us today. God has not changed. **Hebrews 13:8 Jesus Christ, the same yesterday and today and forever** (yes, Jesus is God). We are accountable to what is stated in the Bible. We are called to pay attention to the time and space we are now living. An example of those paying attention in their day were the sons of Issachar.

1 Chronicles 12:32a And of the sons of Issachar, having understanding of the times, to know what Israel should do.

The sons of Issachar are one the twelve tribes of the nation of Israel. Issachar is a son of Jacob (**Genesis 30:18**). His name in Hebrew means "he will bring a reward." The sons of Issachar are the descendants. These sons read the Word. They knew what the times had to offer because they read and believed in God's promises through His Word. Knowing what God says in His word will bring a reward. Read it!

The discussion of "when" this rapture event takes place has no bearing on one's salvation. A person is not destined for the Lake of Fire if they do not understand the timing of the rapture event.

Again, if people who hold to any of these rapture positions believe that Christ died for sins and was resurrected from the dead…Heaven bound. All rapture positions are likely members of the body of Christ. A pastor I know has made a common sense statement. "Good men can respectfully disagree."

Again, I will be up front. I hold to a Pre Tribulation Rapture position with conditions. I think the season of the event is knowable. I will argue the day or two of the event is knowable (little hint). The question is the year of the event. That is tricky.

This is the conclusion I have come to after reading and re reading the text over a period of 20 plus years. I am not telling anybody what to think. I am not telling anybody they are wrong. Dogmatism in opinion solves nothing. Because somebody stomps their foot harder and yells louder does not result in a change of mind and thinking.

Be a Berean. Do not take my word or anybody else's word. Search, read, study.

Acts 17:11 Now these were more noble-minded than those in Thessalonica, for they received the word with great eagerness, examining the Scriptures daily *to see* whether these things were so.

Chapter 5
Israel and the Church

There seems to be a lot of disorder between the concepts of the nation Israel and the body of Christ, the church. If one gets this concept wrong there will be confusion in understanding prophecy as well the Bible. Understanding of the Scriptures will take different paths pending one's view of the church and Israel. Some people take the view Israel and the church are different. Others believe that Israel messed up so bad, God gave up on Israel and replaced the nation with the church, the body of Christ, or spiritual Israel.

A simple, clean definition of Replacement Theology is provided by Matt Slick of https://carm.org/questions-replacement-theology.

Replacement theology is the teaching that the Christian church has replaced national Israel regarding the plan, purpose, and promises of God.

This line of thinking is also called Supersessionism. These folks believe the church is the fulfillment of Judaism. If Jews do not believe in Jesus, they are out. In other words, non-believing Israel has been superseded by the church. No kingdom for you…

The practical results include Israel no longer being God's chosen people and nation. The geographical land promised and designated in the Middle East would belong to the church instead of a group of people living in what is modern day Israel and surrounding countries. The covenants in the Old Testament to Abraham and Moses would be null and void.

Replacement Theology makes God a liar. God's view on this topic as well as any other has not changed. He cannot change. God is immutable. This aspect of His character is defined in the Old Testament.

Malachi 3:6 "For I, the LORD, do not change; therefore you, O sons of Jacob, are not consumed.

This same concept is noted in the New Testament.

James 1:17 Every good thing given and every perfect gift is from above, coming down from the Father of lights, with whom there is no variation or shifting shadow.

The fact that God does not change should be reassurance that what He says is true. God keeps His word and His promises.

Hebrews 13:8 Jesus Christ *is* the same yesterday and today and forever.

Both Israel and the church have different origins and beginnings.

The promise of God's nation started in the plain of Shinar in what is modern day Iraq. Abram was minding his own business in Ur. Then God revealed Himself to this man. God made several promises to Abram.

The first promise was to give Abram some land.

Genesis 12:1e To the land which I will show you;

The second item was the promise to be a great nation.

Genesis 12:2a And I will make you a great nation,

And the last promise to Abram was blessing. Five times a form of the term "bless" is used. Abram and anyone in the world from that point forward who associates with him or his offspring positively, blessing from God!

The Hebrew word for "bless" is **barakah.**

Genesis 12:2b-3 "And I will <u>bless</u> you, and make your name great; and so you shall be a <u>blessing</u>; and I will <u>bless</u> those who <u>bless</u> you, and the one who curses you I will curse. And in you all the families of the earth will be <u>blessed</u>."

It was not enough to tell Abram. God made a contract or covenant with him for all time. **Genesis 15** provides the details of the covenant. A direct son was promised to Abram. The number to come from his body would number the stars in the heavens. Animals and birds with specifications were part of the covenant.

God put Abram to sleep and sealed the deal Himself. The contract is on God to be completed. Abram did not have to do anything, he was out cold. Frankly, he would not have been able to do anything because of his mental status. It was dark and Abram was scared to death. There is nothing any fallen man can do. The responsibility belongs to God.

Genesis 15:12 Now when the sun was going down, a deep sleep fell upon Abram; and behold, terror *and* great darkness fell upon him.

This is the original land grant promised to the future nation Israel. These are the land boundaries of Israel's future. This configuration has never been realized. This calls for the geography of Israel to stretch from the Nile River in Egypt to the Euphrates River in Iraq. One could argue if this includes the Arabian Peninsula or not. Now this sounds impossible in today's world and geo-political climate. Can you imagine the uproar if this was proposed at the United Nations? But, there will be a land for peace deal when Jesus returns. It will look something like this.

Genesis 15:18-21 On that day the LORD made a covenant with Abram, saying, "To your descendants I have given this land, From the river of Egypt as far as the great river, the river Euphrates: the Kenite and the Kenizzite and the Kadmonite and the Hittite and the Perizzite and the Rephaim and the Amorite and the Canaanite and the Girgashite and the Jebusite."

The key issue for Abram is the same issue we have today. Do we believe God? Do we take what God says seriously? Does God really mean it? In Abram's case, did he believe the promises of things to come? Today in the 21st century, do we believe the good news of Jesus Christ? His death, burial, and resurrection is the issue for our salvation.

Genesis 15:6 Then he believed in the Lord; and He reckoned it to him as righteousness.

So…will God make Israel great again? Over twenty times in the book of **Genesis** alone, God stated His covenant with the offspring of Abram is an eternal and everlasting promise. He made the claim to Abram (later Abraham), Isaac, Jacob (later Israel) and his descendants.

Will God keep His promise to Israel in regards to the land grant? In the book <u>Toward an Old Testament Theology</u>, Walter Kaiser commented, "sixty nine times the writer of Deutoronomy repeated the pledge that Israel would one day 'possess' and 'inherit' the land promised to her." (p. 124-5).

Is God going to bless the world through Israel? Do you believe the record?

Eventually the offspring of Abram would become the promised nation. This is the story of the birth of a nation. The verses below are how the man named Jacob had his name changed to Israel. The nation Israel would come from this man. This is a brief history, present, and future of God's chosen nation.

Genesis 32:24-28 And Jacob was left alone. And a man wrestled with him until the breaking of the day. When the man saw that he did not prevail against Jacob, he touched his hip socket, and Jacob's hip was put out of joint as he wrestled with him. Then he said, "Let me go, for the day has broken." But Jacob said, "I will not let you go unless you bless me." And he said to him, "What is your name?" And he said, "Jacob." Then he said, "Your name shall no longer be called Jacob, but Israel, for you have striven with God and with men, and have prevailed."

In the Hebrew, Jacob or **Ya`aqob** means "heel holder" or "supplanter". It can also mean he cheats or deceives. Jacob was given this name because of the events at his birth.

Genesis 25:26a Afterward his brother came forth with his hand holding on to Esau's heel, so his name was called Jacob…

This name accurately describes Jacob. He cheated and deceived his brother Esau for his inheritance. The deceiver met his match in his future father in law, Laban. See **Genesis 29-31** for the complete details with Laban the master manipulator.

God changed Jacob's name to Israel. In the Hebrew, Israel or **Yisra'el** means "God prevails". Per Holman's Bible Dictionary, Israel means God strives, God rules, God heals, or he strives against God.

Genesis 32:28 Then he said, "Your name shall no longer be called Jacob, but Israel, for you have striven with God and with men, and have prevailed."

The verse above has proven to be prophetic for nation Israel. The country struggled against Egypt and was held captive for 400 years. God delivered His people out of slavery and bondage in the Book of **Exodus.**

God's chosen people were taken captive by Tiglath-Pileser and the Assyrian Empire. Nebuchadnezzar led the Babylonians and plundered Jerusalem. Those who survived were taken back to Babylon. Israel was under Persian rule after they conquered Babylon.

They were dispersed throughout the world in the first century at the hands of the Roman Empire. They survived the Spanish Inquisition in the late 1400's. Hitler attempted to exterminate the Jewish people during the middle of the 20th century in World War II.

Israel was reborn as a country in a day in 1948. The rebirth of Israel in one day was prophesied in **Isaiah 66:8-9.**

Isaiah 66:8-9 "Who has heard such a thing? Who has seen such things? Can a land be born in one day? Can a nation be brought forth all at once? As soon as Zion travailed, she also brought forth her sons. Shall I bring to the point of birth and not give delivery?" says the LORD. "Or shall I who gives delivery shut *the womb?"* **says your God.**

The same promise of **Ezekiel 37** and the vision of the valley of dry bones was fulfilled. Israel is a nation again. The fact Israel is a nation again defies history. Name one other country who disappeared for about 2,000 years and resurrected into being from the past.

Arguably, there is yet another name coming for the people and nation who are currently known as Israel. God Himself will make the change. The Bible says that name will be **Hephzibah**.

Isaiah 62:1-4 For Zion's sake I will not keep silent, and for Jerusalem's sake I will not keep quiet, until her righteousness goes forth like brightness, and her salvation like a torch that is burning. The nations will see your righteousness, and all kings your glory; and you will be called by a new name which the mouth of the LORD will designate. You will also be a crown of beauty in the hand of the LORD, and a royal diadem in the hand of your God. It will no longer be said to you, "Forsaken," nor to your land will it any longer be said, "Desolate"; but you will be called, "My delight is in her," and your land, "Married"; for the LORD delights in you, and *to Him* your land will be married.

The name Hephzibah is noted one other place in the Bible. She was the mother of King Manasseh and queen to King Hezekiah.

2 Kings 21:1 Manasseh was twelve years old when he became king, and he reigned fifty-five years in Jerusalem; and his mother's name was Hephzibah.

Hephzibah in the original Hebrew means: **My delight is in her.**

The land will undergo a name change as well, "married" or **Beulah**. Per Strong's **Beulah** means: to marry, rule over, possess, own, be lord (husband) over. The relationship between God and the land is that of a marriage covenant. Some know the term from the southern hymn "**Sweet Beulah Land**".

Along the way, God has healed and preserved His chosen people. And they have wrestled with Him. God prevails. For the nations hostile to Israel who say, "Israel will be no more…" They are correct. Israel will no longer wrestle with God or with the nations of humanity. The struggle will end. God and Israel will prevail. God's delight will be in His chosen people, Hephzibah… and the land, Beulah.

Amos 9:15 I will also plant them on their land, and they will not again be rooted out from their land which I have given them," Says the LORD your God.

Beginning of the church…

The church or the body of Jesus Christ has ties to the Old Testament Mosaic Law and God's Appointed Holiday of Shavuot. I realize this will be blasphemy in some circles of theology reading this. Hear me out before going ballistic and deeming me a heretic. God has a plan down to the day!

The Law was given on Mount Sinai to Moses roughly 1,600 years before Christ. In the Old Testament and in the Hebrew, this God appointed holiday is referred to as **Shavuot**. The word means: weeks. **Shavuot** or the Feast of Weeks is a memorial of God giving Moses and Israel the Torah. Hebraic belief is redemption from Egyptian slavery was not complete until they received the instruction or teaching. The holiday is one of God's seven appointed holidays. Nation Israel honored **Shavuot**, the Feast of Weeks, every year.

Provisions for the holiday include two loaves of bread, sacrificial lambs, a bull, two rams, a goat, and a drink offering of wine. God gives directions on how to make bread. Specifications for choosing livestock are given. God loves the smell of grilled meats by fire. Toasted bread smells great. The holiday is also a day of rest with no work, a Sabbath. And He wants His people to do this celebration and exercise it every year on the same day. Is God being unreasonable? He offers a holiday with grilled meats, toasted bread, and alcohol. It is an outdoor party in the late spring around a camp fire. Celebrate the harvest and give thanks to God. Road trip to Jerusalem!!!

See the Scripture for the complete details.

Leviticus 23:17-21 You shall bring in from your dwelling places two *loaves* of bread for a wave offering, made of two-tenths *of an*

ephah; they shall be of a fine flour, baked with leaven as first fruits to the Lord. Along with the bread you shall present seven one year old male lambs without defect, and a bull of the herd and two rams; they are to be a burnt offering to the Lord, with their grain offering and their drink offerings, an offering by fire of a soothing aroma to the Lord. You shall also offer one male goat for a sin offering and two male lambs one year old for a sacrifice of peace offerings. The priest shall then wave them with the bread of the first fruits for a wave offering with two lambs before the Lord; they are to be holy to the Lord for the priest. On this same day you shall make a proclamation as well; you are to have a holy convocation. You shall do no laborious work. It is to be a perpetual statute in all your dwelling places throughout your generations.

Shavuot or the Feast of the Harvest is one of the three holidays where Jewish men are required to come to Jerusalem. The other two holidays are the Feast of Unleavened Bread and the Feast of the Ingathering (Tabernacles or the Feast of Booths). The men were to make their presentation and sacrifice before God at the Temple.

Exodus 23:14-17 "Three times a year you shall celebrate a feast to Me. You shall observe the Feast of Unleavened Bread; for seven days you are to eat unleavened bread, as I commanded you, at the appointed time in the month Abib, for in it you came out of Egypt. And none shall appear before Me empty-handed. Also *you shall observe* the Feast of the Harvest *of* the first fruits of your labors *from* what you sow in the field; also the Feast of the Ingathering at the end of the year when you gather in *the fruit of* your labors from the field. Three times a year all your males shall appear before the Lord God."

Eating and drinking dairy products are part of the celebration of **Shavuot**. Many think the custom of dairy products is in reference to Bible verses referring to a promised land flowing with milk and honey. See the example below.

Exodus 3:8a "So I have come down to deliver them from the power of the Egyptians, and to bring them up from that land to a good and spacious land, to a land flowing with milk and honey...

As stated in the **Leviticus** passage, **the Feast of Weeks** is seven weeks after Passover. It is a celebration of the completed grain harvest. The holiday is also a celebration of God giving the Torah (instruction or law) to nation Israel. Because of this, **Shavuot** is considered as the beginning or birth of Judaism.

Fast forward to 33 AD. Nation Israel has been celebrating and living God's Appointed Spring holidays. Jesus Christ, the Passover Lamb, had been sacrificed. He was the buried Unleavened Bread. Christ is the First Fruits of the resurrection. Then fifty days later...

It is seven weeks after the death of the sacrificial lamb, Jesus. Nation Israel is celebrating and living the holiday. **Shavuot** or **Pentecost** is also the day God the Father gave God the Holy Spirit. Because of this, **Pentecost** is considered the beginning or the birth of the church or the body of believers in Jesus Christ.

Acts 2:1 When the day of Pentecost had come, they (apostles) **were all together in one place.**

Acts 2:4 And they were all filled with the Holy Spirit and began to speak with other tongues, as the Spirit was giving them utterance.

In the Greek New Testament, **Shavuot** (Hebrew) is translated as πεντεκοστε/**pentekoste** (Greek). Per Strong's Concordance, it means: the fiftieth day; the second of the three great Jewish feasts, celebrated at Jerusalem yearly, the seventh week after the Passover, in grateful recognition of the completed harvest. We have transliterated the word to **Pentecost** (English).

This is the day promised by Jesus of the giving of the Holy Spirit.

John 14:26 But the Helper, the Holy Spirit, whom the Father will send in My name, He will teach you all things, and bring to your remembrance all that I said to you.

Acts 2:38 Peter *said* to them, "Repent, and each of you be baptized in the name of Jesus Christ for the forgiveness of your sins; and you will receive the gift of the Holy Spirit…"

Shavuot, Feast of Weeks, Feast of the Harvest, and Pentecost are synonymous. Shavuot is often associated with God giving the Torah, the birth of Judaism. Pentecost is often associated with God giving the Holy Spirit, the birth of the church. God chose His appointed holiday to reveal aspects of who He is.

The Greek word for "church" is εκκλεσια/**ekklesia.** It means: an assembly, congregation; the whole body of Christian believers. People called out from the world and to God, the mystical body of Christ; the universal body of believers whom God calls out from the world and into His eternal kingdom. Strong's Concordance

Vine's Expository Dictionary of New Testament Words breaks down the word εκκλεσια/**ekklesia.** The following definition and contexts are provided by the dictionary.

εκκλεσια/**ekklesia:** from **ek**, "out of;" and **klesis**, "a calling" (**kaleo**, "to call"). The word is used in many different ways in the New Testament. Below are some examples of contexts and usage of the word.

In **Acts 19:39, ekklesia** was used among the Greeks of a body of citizens "gathered" to discuss the affairs of state. In the September it is used to designate the "gathering" of Israel, summoned for any definite purpose, or a "gathering" regarded as representative of the whole nation.

Acts 19:39 But if you want anything beyond this, it shall be settled in the lawful <u>assembly</u>.

In **Acts 7:38 ekklesia** is used of the nation Israel. Here the word is translated as "congregation".

Acts 7:38 This is the one who was in the <u>congregation</u> in the wilderness together with the angel who was speaking to him on Mount Sinai, and *who was* with our fathers; and he received living oracles to pass on to you.

The example below presents the term **ekklesia** as a mob in Ephesus. Here the word is translated "assembly".

Acts 19:32 So then, some were shouting one thing and some another, for the <u>assembly</u> was in confusion and the majority did not know for what reason they had come together.

The focus of the term **ekklesia** in this book is on the body of believers in Jesus Christ. The term is used at least 111 occurrences in the New Testament. The majority of the instances, it is translated as "church".

The first time the word **ekklesia** is used in the New Testament is by Jesus Himself.

Matthew 16:18 I also say to you that you are Peter, and upon this rock I will build My <u>church</u>; and the gates of Hades will not overpower it.

www.mf.no/bibelprog/vines?word=%AFt0000173

Jesus uses the word **ekklesia.** Christ states He is the person doing the construction. He also claims the church is His. "**I will build My church.**" -Jesus.

Embedded in this verse, **"…and the gates of Hades will not overpower it."** -Jesus.

Some would argue this as a pre tribulation rapture statement. Hell and the antichrist are not going to win against the church or the body of Christ. Hell is not stronger and will not prevail against the church.

Compare this statement by Jesus in **Matthew 16:18** against **Revelation 13:7** and **Daniel 7:21**.

Revelation 13:7 It was also given to him to make war with the saints and to overcome them, and authority over every tribe and people and tongue and nation was given to him…

The reference to "him" is the antichrist. He is allowed to "overcome". Conquer is the idea expressed in the Greek language. The antichrist is given authority to do whatever he wants. This guy is a universal dictator and acts with a heavy hand over the tribulation saints.

Daniel 7:21 I kept looking, and that horn was waging war with the saints and overpowering them…

In the Bible, horns are equated with kings, kingdoms, and leaders. This was the case in the writings of the Old Testament and the New Testament. Daniel's dream in **Daniel 7** is consistent with verses in **Revelation 13** and **17.** The language regarding beasts and horns is consistent.

This section of **Daniel 7** is in the Aramaic language. Interesting observation, this section of **Daniel** that focuses on gentile worldly kingdoms is in Aramaic and not the original Hebrew. The Aramaic states the antichrist is making war. He is winning and prevailing against the saints.

The church is in Heaven as of **Revelation 4** before the tribulation starts. The context of **Revelation 13** and **Daniel 7:21** is on Earth.

People are being persecuted and killed by the antichrist. These are the people who did not believe in Jesus Christ at the time of the resurrection and rapture. They were left behind and came to understand the truth about Christ later. The Tribulation saints are a different group of people than the church.

The church or the body of Jesus Christ is not overcome by Hell, Satan, the beast, or false prophet. Jesus said.

The term **ekklesia** is generally translated as the church, the body of Jesus Christ. Scripture does the best job of defining the idea. See the three examples below.

Colossians 1:18a He is also head of the body, the church...

He is Jesus Christ.

Ephesians 1:22b-23 and gave Him as head over all things to the church, which is His body, the fullness of Him who fills all in all.

Ephesians 5:23 For the husband is the head of the wife, as Christ also is the head of the church, He Himself *being* the Savior of the body.

There are many other examples in the New Testament where the church is described as a body of believers in Jesus Christ (**Acts 20:28; 1 Corinthians 1:2; Galatians 1:13; 1 Thessalonians 1:1; 2 Thessalonians 1:1; 1 Timothy 3:5**).

The church is not a building. The church is not nation Israel. The church is a body of believers attached to the head, Jesus Christ.

The body of Jesus Christ (the church) and Israel are two distinct, separate entities with two different destinations. God spends more time in the Bible talking about the destination of Israel as compared to the church.

First, we will look at the destiny of Israel. Ultimately Israel will be restored to the greatness God promised to Abram in **Genesis 12**. Israel will be a blessing to all nations. Jesus will rule His kingdom from Jerusalem, Israel for a thousand years and into eternity. But before Israel gets there, difficult times will come upon the nation and the world as have never been before. Jesus makes the comment this will be the worst time in the history of the earth. However, He will preserve a remnant.

Matthew 24:21-22 For then there will be a great tribulation, such as has not occurred since the beginning of the world until now, nor ever will. Unless those days had been cut short, no life would have been saved; but for the sake of the elect those days will be cut short.

Unfortunately for the nation of Israel a set of seven or seven years remains on God's time table. Daniel's people are fellow Israeli's. Daniel's holy city is Jerusalem. The verse from the prophet is very clear. Israel's future is deal with sin and end it. Judgment comes first then restoration and peace.

Daniel 9:24 Seventy weeks have been decreed for your people and your holy city, to finish the transgression, to make an end of sin, to make atonement for iniquity, to bring in everlasting righteousness, to seal up vision and prophecy and to anoint the most holy *place.*

This period is known as the "Time of Jacob's Trouble." The concept of Jacob's trouble comes from the prophet **Jeremiah 30**. God makes it very clear to Israel. Judgment is coming, but I will not forget you. There are many examples in the chapter. Here is one of the verses.

Jeremiah 30:11 "For I am with you," declares the Lord, "to save you; for I will destroy completely all the nations where I have scattered you, only I will not destroy you completely. But I will chasten you justly and will by no means leave you unpunished."

The Apostle Paul in the New Testament book of **Romans** makes it very clear. God is not finished with nation Israel. He makes this statement writing to members of the church in Rome. His writings included the idea of Israel's election, Israel's rejection, and Israel's future restoration. Paul is in serious angst and agony regarding his fellow countrymen. He would go to Hell for Israel. God has not kicked Israel to the curb let alone replaced them with the church or any other group of people or nation.

Romans 9:3-4 For I could wish that I myself were accursed, *separated* from Christ for the sake of my brethren, my kinsmen according to the flesh, who are Israelites, to whom belongs the adoption as sons, and the glory and the covenants and the giving of the Law and the *temple* service and the promises...

The Apostle Paul is emphatic. There is *NO* way God has broken His promise to His people and nation, Israel. The idea is consistent in the Old Testament and New Testament. God has not changed His mind.

Romans 11:1-11:2 I say then, God has not rejected His people, has He? May it never be! For I too am an Israelite, a descendant of Abraham, of the tribe of Benjamin. God has not rejected His people whom He foreknew. Or do you not know what the Scripture says in *the passage about* **Elijah, how he pleads with God against Israel?**

Malachi 3:6 "For I, the Lord, do not change; therefore you, O sons of Jacob, are not consumed."

Today in the early 21st century, Israel is back in the land and a nation as prophesied. Israel has resurrected as a nation. This time, they will not reject their Messiah. The statement below is becoming more of a reality as time passes. There are Jews who believe in Jesus and the number is growing. The world will ultimately receive blessing.

11:15 For if their rejection is the reconciliation of the world, what will *their* **acceptance be but life from the dead?**

Romans 11:26 and so all Israel will be saved; just as it is written, "The Deliverer will come from Zion, He will remove ungodliness from Jacob."

Focus on the word "saved". It is the Greek word σοζο/sozo. The word is defined as to save, keep safe and sound, to rescue from danger or destruction; one (from injury or peril); to save a suffering one (from perishing), i.e. one suffering from disease, to make well, heal, restore to health (Strong's Concordance).

The tense of the verb is future. The verse is prophetic. Israel will be spared and preserved in the future. At the time of the writing, Israel had yet to be dispersed to the world let alone regathered back to the land. The nation will not be destroyed.

Every Old Testament prophet except Jonah discusses the restoration of the nation of Israel. This promise is not made to the church. The Abrahamic Covenant is for Israel. Keep in mind, the church was not on the scene when the prophets spoke to their people, Israel and their city Jerusalem.

Isaiah 65:9 "I will bring forth offspring from Jacob, and an heir of My mountains from Judah; even My chosen ones shall inherit it, and My servants will dwell there."

Jeremiah 30:3 For behold, days are coming, declares the Lord, "when I will restore the fortunes of My people Israel and Judah." The Lord says, "I will also bring them back to the land that I gave to their forefathers and they shall possess it."

Ezekiel Chapter 34

Daniel 7:14 And to Him was given dominion, glory and a kingdom, that all the peoples, nations and *men of every* language might serve Him. His dominion is an everlasting dominion which will not pass away; and His kingdom is one which will not be destroyed.

Hosea Chapter 2

Joel 2:19 The Lord will answer and say to His people, "Behold, I am going to send you grain, new wine and oil, and you will be satisfied *in full* with them; and I will never again make you a reproach among the nations."

Amos 9:14 "Also I will restore the captivity of My people Israel, and they will rebuild the ruined cities and live *in them;* they will also plant vineyards and drink their wine, and make gardens and eat their fruit."

Obadiah 1:17 "But on Mount Zion there will be those who escape, and it will be holy. And the house of Jacob will possess their possessions.

Micah 2:12 "I will surely assemble all of you, Jacob, I will surely gather the remnant of Israel. I will put them together like sheep in the fold; like a flock in the midst of its pasture they will be noisy with men."

Nahum 2:2 For the Lord will restore the splendor of Jacob like the splendor of Israel, even though devastators have devastated them and destroyed their vine branches.

Habakkuk Chapter 3

Zephaniah 3:20 "At that time I will bring you in, even at the time when I gather you together; Indeed, I will give you renown and praise among all the peoples of the earth, when I restore your fortunes before your eyes," says the Lord.

Haggai 2:9 "The latter glory of this house will be greater than the former," says the Lord of hosts, "and in this place I will give peace," declares the Lord of hosts.

Zechariah Chapter 8

Malachi 3:12 "All the nations will call you blessed, for you shall be a delightful land," says the Lord of hosts."

I would challenge any one to show one place where God states he replaced Israel with the church. Examine the Scriptures. Where is it?

The church is not the nation Israel. Members of the church are to rule and reign with Jesus Christ. Jesus Himself makes it very clear the church and Israel are different. The followers of Christ will judge Israel.

Matthew 19:28 Jesus said to them, "Truly I tell you, in the renewal of all things, when the Son of Man sits on His glorious throne, you who have followed Me will also sit on twelve thrones, judging the twelve tribes of Israel."

2 Timothy 2:12a if we endure, we will also reign with him...

The reminder of ruling with Christ is the last message He gives to the churches in the book of **Revelation**.

Revelation 3:21 He who overcomes, I will grant to him to sit down with Me on My throne, as I also overcame and sat down with My Father on His throne.

The church will even judge angels as well as the world. Paul explains this in his first letter to the body of believers in Corinth.

1 Corinthians 6:2-3 Or do you not know that the saints will judge the world? If the world is judged by you, are you not competent to constitute the smallest law courts? Do you not

know that we will judge angels? How much more matters of this life?

Until these things happen, our destination as a member of the church is one of two places. Obviously, believers in Christ who are alive are on earth. If we die before the Lord comes for His bride, then we go to be with Jesus Christ.

2 Corinthians 5:8 we are of good courage, I say, and prefer rather to be absent from the body and to be at home with the Lord.

Members of the body of Christ who have physically died are said to be "asleep". Sleeping is not an eternal state. At some point, we get up and awake. A physically dead body is resting. The soul and spirit are with the Lord as noted in the verse from **2 Corinthians**. Bodily death is not eternal. A section in **1 Thessalonians 4** captures the concept of sleep and order of events for members of the body of Christ. This section is addressed to the church, not Israel. Notice, the letter is written to those "in Jesus". Israel was not and currently is not "in Jesus".

1 Thessalonians 4:13-17 But we do not want you to be uninformed, brethren, about those who are asleep, so that you will not grieve as do the rest who have no hope. For if we believe that Jesus died and rose again, even so God will bring with Him those who have fallen asleep in Jesus. For this we say to you by the word of the Lord, that we who are alive and remain until the coming of the Lord, will not precede those who have fallen asleep. For the Lord Himself will descend from heaven with a shout, with the voice of *the* archangel and with the trumpet of God, and the dead in Christ will rise first. Then we who are alive and remain will be caught up together with them in the clouds to meet the Lord in the air, and so we shall always be with the Lord.

Let's look at an overview of the book of **Revelation**. The point of the exercise to look at the physical location of the church and Israel in time and space. When and where are nation Israel and the church located.

Before we get started, an observation in vocabulary for the book. The Greek word for church εκκλεσια/ekklesia is mentioned 19 times in **Revelation chapters 1-3**. The word εκκλεσια/ekklesia is not used again until **Revelation 22:16**. The context of verse is a reminder. This is a message to the churches. It is warning information. A serious storm is coming.

Revelation 22:16 "I, Jesus, have sent My angel to testify to you these things for the churches. I am the root and the descendant of David, the bright morning star."

In **Revelation 1**, The Apostle John is taking information and writing down the record from the Island Patmos on Earth. Patmos is an island in the Aegean Sea. The word "Patmos" means: my killing. The Apostle John was sentenced to the island of "my killing". Where are you going? My killing.

Patmos is a small island approximately 10 miles by 6 miles. It is a rocky island. Tradition has John receiving the "**Revelation**" in a cave on the south side of the island.

Scholars generally believe **Revelation** was written during the reign of the Roman emperor Domitian. He ruled from 81-96 AD. The early church writers Irenaeus, Eusebius, Jerome and others indicated John was sent to Patmos by Domitian in 95 AD. John was released 1 1/2 years later.

Historically Patmos was controlled by the Ottoman Empire. Today the island belongs to modern day Greece.

Revelation 1:9 I, John, your brother and fellow partaker in the tribulation and kingdom and perseverance *which are* in Jesus, was on the island called Patmos because of the word of God and the testimony of Jesus.

Revelation chapters 2 and 3 are written to seven churches on Earth in what is 21st century country Turkey. It would appear John sent one "book" or epistle to the seven churches. The book was sent from the island of Patmos. The order of the seven churches listed is geographical and clockwise in nature. The first stop on the mainland of Turkey was Ephesus. Next, the letter would have gone north to Smyrna. The third stop was north in Pergamum. Following Pergamum to the east and a bit south was Thyatira. The fifth stop to the south would have been Sardis. A jog to the east and the letter stopped in Philadelphia. The last stop to the south and east was Laodicea.

Four of the seven churches in Revelation have references to Satan. Jesus is the one talking directly to the churches. Jesus got His information from God the Father (**Revelation 1**). This is not conjecture. The churches with the reference to Satan are: Smyrna, Pergamum, Thyatira, and Philadelphia.

Per the comments of Jesus, Satan clearly has a foot hold in Turkey to the churches in **Revelation**. Satan has a religious system and structures in place in this geographical area on Earth. If Satan's home land is modern day Turkey, would it make sense for him to establish his kingdom with his minions here?

Revelation 1:11 saying, "Write in a book what you see, and send *it* to the seven churches: to Ephesus and to Smyrna and to Pergamum and to Thyatira and to Sardis and to Philadelphia and to Laodicea." -Jesus

Revelation chapters 4 and 5 have a change in location. The scene has changed to the throne room in Heaven. John now finds himself in Heaven.

Revelation 4:2 Immediately I was in the Spirit; and behold, a throne was standing in heaven...

The first thing he notices is God the Father's appearance on His throne.

Revelation 4:2b-3 and One sitting on the throne. And He who was sitting *was* like a jasper stone and a sardius in appearance; and *there was* a rainbow around the throne, like an emerald in appearance.

John's next observation appears to be the church. Language and symbols presented are consistent with a description of the body of Christ.

Revelation 4:4 Around the throne *were* twenty-four thrones; and upon the thrones *I saw* twenty-four elders sitting, clothed in white garments, and golden crowns on their heads.

"Elders" were sitting on thrones. The Greek word for "elders" is πρεσβυτεροσ/**presbuteros.** These are among the Christians who presided over the assemblies or churches (Strong's Concordance). This is the same term used throughout the New Testament for leaders in the local church.

Leadership is being shared with the One. The reality of ruling with the Son and Father is being observed by John. From this point forward in **Revelation**, members of the body of Christ are referred to in a leadership capacity, an elder.

The elders are wearing white garments. Members of the church wear white garments. This is the fulfillment of the promise given by Jesus in **Revelation 3:5** to those who have victory in Him. In **Revelation 3**, the believers were on Earth. In **Revelation 4**, they are in Heaven.

Revelation 3:5 He who overcomes will thus be clothed in white garments; and I will not erase his name from the book of life, and I will confess his name before My Father and before His angels.

Jesus is introduced in **Revelation 5** as a lion and a lamb. He keeps the company of elders in the chapter. They are all in Heaven. Remember, judgment or God's wrath has yet to start on Earth.

Revelation 5:5 and one of the elders said to me, "Stop weeping; behold, the <u>Lion</u> that is from the tribe of Judah, the Root of David, has overcome so as to open the book and its seven seals."

Notice the language of the church leadership and elders. They are in Heaven. Prayers have ascended from Earth from the "saints". These are two different groups in two different locations. People who are left behind (saints) after the church ascended to Heaven have already come to believe in Jesus Christ. The resurrection and rapture of the church will have a spiritual impact on people who did not believe at the time of the event. This group of people is called "saints" not the church. The Greek word for "saints" is ηαγιοσ/**hagios**. The saints are the most holy and sacred thing left on Earth (Strong's Concordance).

Revelation 5:8 When He had taken the book, the four living creatures and the twenty-four elders fell down before the Lamb, each one holding a harp and golden bowls full of incense, which are the prayers of the saints.

Revelation chapter 6 introduces judgment on Earth with the four horsemen of the Apocalypse. It is not until **chapter 7** that Israel is mentioned. Israel is located on Earth while judgment is taking place. The twelve tribes of Israel are reintroduced in sets of 12,000 for a total of 144,000.

At the same time, the church and elders remain in Heaven. Saints on Earth are present and dying. Note the saints who die on Earth join the God the Father, God the Son, the elders and angels in Heaven.

Revelation 7:9-11 After these things I looked, and behold, a great multitude which no one could count, from every nation and *all* tribes and peoples and tongues, standing before the throne and before the Lamb, clothed in white robes, and palm branches *were* in their hands; and they cry out with a loud voice, saying, "Salvation to our God who sits on the throne, and to the Lamb." And all the angels were standing around the throne and *around* the elders and the four living creatures; and they fell on their faces before the throne and worshiped God...

Judgment continues on Earth with the introduction of the two witnesses in **Revelation 11**. Satan is thrown out of Heaven and down to Earth by the angel Michael in **chapter 12**. The antichrist and the false prophet enter the scene on Earth in **Revelation 13**.

In **Revelation 14**, Jesus the Lamb has moved from Heaven to Earth. His location is Mount Zion or Jerusalem. 144,000 Israelis have joined Him for choir practice. Meanwhile back in Heaven, the elders or the church is singing before the throne of God the Father. Israel is on Earth. The church is in Heaven. The two entities are different in name and physical location in the context of the chapter. The text could not be any clearer. Replacement Theology or Supersessionism is a myth.

Judgment continues on Earth through **Revelation 18** then the setting changes to Heaven in **chapter 19**. The Lamb and His bride the church are married in Heaven. Then Christ and His army descend to Earth. The beast and his troops decide to engage the King of Kings. The result of the antichrist and the false prophet is the lake of fire on Earth. Satan has a 1,000 year time out chained up in the abyss. Israel is on Earth and ready to usher in the kingdom.

The church is destined for resurrection and rapture before Israel has a seven year period of judgment. The church returns to earth to rule and reign with the King of Kings over the world through nation Israel for 1,000 years and into eternity.

Chapter 6
The Second Coming of Christ

The rapture and the second coming of Jesus Christ are two distinct, separate events. A look at the Bible verses surrounding both events indicates the unique nature of both events.

Location, Location, Location

For starters, the rapture takes place in the air and in the clouds. Jesus does not descend to earth.

1 Thessalonians 4:16-17 For the Lord Himself will descend from heaven with a shout, with the voice of *the* archangel and with the trumpet of God, and the dead in Christ will rise first. Then we who are alive and remain will be caught up together with them in the clouds to meet the Lord in the air, and so we shall always be with the Lord.

With the second coming of Christ, He physically returns to the Earth. A specific location of the Mount of Olives east of Jerusalem is given.

Zechariah 14:4 In that day His feet will stand on the Mount of Olives, which is in front of Jerusalem on the east; and the Mount of Olives will be split in its middle from east to west by a very large valley, so that half of the mountain will move toward the north and the other half toward the south.

Revelation 19:11-21 describes the return of Jesus to the Earth. His physical presence is noted in **verse 19**. The antichrist, armies, and nations of the world are gathered to declare war on Jesus. The Lord cleans their clock at the end of this passage.

Revelation 19:19 And I saw the beast and the kings of the earth and their armies assembled to make war against Him who sat on the horse and against His army.

Timing

There are no signs or precursor events for the gathering of believers at the resurrection and rapture. I personally believe the rapture takes place in the fall around God's Appointments. The issue is the specific year. There are subtle clues in the figurative language and Hebrew culture of the text that lead me to this conclusion. When the bride of Christ is removed, the tribulation will start. The Apostle Paul is clear in **2 Thessalonians**. The restrainer or the Holy Spirit indwelled in believers is currently keeping order. The Holy Spirit is keeping the antichrist from being known the world.

2 Thessalonians 2:6-7 And you know what restrains him now, so that in his time he will be revealed. For the mystery of lawlessness is already at work; only he who now restrains *will do so* until he is taken out of the way.

The antichrist is the first character revealed by the Lamb or Jesus Christ in **Revelation 6**. The lawless one revealed initiates the start of the Great Tribulation.

Revelation 6:2 I looked, and behold, a white horse, and he who sat on it had a bow; and a crown was given to him, and he went out conquering and to conquer.

The timing of the second coming is knowable. Jesus will reveal Himself on Earth a second time at the end of the seven year Tribulation. Scripture tells us Christ is seven years away from the start of the Tribulation.

Daniel 9:27 And he will make a firm covenant with the many for one week, but in the middle of the week he will put a stop to sacrifice and grain offering; and on the wing of abominations *will come* one who makes desolate, even until a complete destruction, one that is decreed, is poured out on the one who makes desolate."

And he will make a firm covenant with the many for one week... The man who brokers the deal will definitively be the man who makes it happen. He will have the personality and be the center of attention. In the Hebrew, he is **gabar:** to prevail, have strength, be strong, be powerful, be mighty, or be great. He forges the alliance, treaty, or pledge. The treaty will be with the many or **rab** in the

Hebrew. This can mean: much, many, great, abundant, or numerous. Middle East peace is going to be a big deal!

The length of the treaty is for "one week" or one **shabuwa`**. A **shabuwa`** is defined as a seven, period of seven (days or years), heptad, or week. This is an expression of how Jews keeps time.

Revelation does not specifically state a seven year period. **Revelation 11:2-3** does give reference to periods of time of 42 months and 1,260 days. Both time periods are 3 1/2 years. Added together, seven years.

Revelation 11:2-3 "Leave out the court which is outside the temple and do not measure it, for it has been given to the nations; and they will tread underfoot the holy city for forty-two months. And I will grant *authority* **to my two witnesses, and they will prophesy for twelve hundred and sixty days, clothed in sackcloth."**

but in the middle of the week he will put a stop to sacrifice and grain offering... The sacrificial system will be reinitiated in the Temple. Today, the only thing preventing the Jews from starting the Temple service is the need for a Temple. See the Temple Mount Institute for details.

www.templeinstitute.org/

www.facebook.com/pages/The-Temple-Institute/22738684968

Halfway through the seven year treaty, the sacrificial system of the Old Testament is halted by the beast in the Temple. And when this happens, get out of Jerusalem immediately! Do not waste time! See **Matthew 24** and **Mark 13** for details.

Matthew 24:15 Jesus confirms the writings of the prophet Daniel. **"Therefore when you see the ABOMINATION OF DESOLATION which was spoken of through Daniel the prophet, standing in the holy place (let the reader understand)..."**

Matthew 24:21 For then there will be a great tribulation, such as has not occurred since the beginning of the world until now, nor ever will. -Jesus.

The antichrist has his day of rule for the last half of the seven year period.

Revelation 13:5 There was given to him a mouth speaking arrogant words and blasphemies, and authority to act for <u>forty-two months</u> was given to him.

How long will the beast or antichrist rule? Scripture makes it perfectly clear, 42 months…

In the original Greek it states: **τεσσαρακοντα/tessarakonta** (40), **καὶ/kai** (and), **δυο/duo** (two), **μεν/men** (months). -Strong's Concordance.

Revelation 11:2 Leave out the court which is outside the temple and do not measure it, for it has been given to the nations; and they will tread underfoot the holy city for <u>forty-two months</u>.

The temple will need to be built and operational for the antichrist/beast to overtake. The gentiles or non-Jews will be in charge for the same time period, 42 months.

This same time period is restated elsewhere in Scripture.

Revelation 12:6 Then the woman fled into the wilderness where she had a place prepared by God, so that there she would be nourished for <u>one thousand two hundred and sixty days</u>. The woman is Israel and she is fleeing from the dragon or Satan. She is protected by God during this time period. God operates on a 30 day lunar calendar. 1,260 days divided by 30 days = 42 months.

Revelation 12:14 But the two wings of the great eagle were given to the woman, so that she could fly into the wilderness to her place, where she was nourished for <u>a time and times and half a time</u>, from the presence of the serpent.

… a time and times and half a time… This is another expression of marking 42 months. The Greek word for time is **καιροσ/kairos**. It means: due measure of time, hence: a fixed and definite time, the time when things are brought to crisis, the decisive epoch waited for, opportune or seasonable time, the right time, a limited period of time. -Strong's Concordance

This expression is noted in **Daniel 7:25. He will speak out against the Most High and wear down the saints of the Highest One, and he will intend to make alterations in times and in law; and they will be given into his hand for <u>a time, times, and half a time.</u>**

It is also in **Daniel 12:7 I heard the man dressed in linen, who was above the waters of the river, as he raised his right hand and his left toward heaven, and swore by Him who lives forever that it would be for <u>a time, times, and half</u> *a time;* and as soon as they finish shattering the power of the holy people, all these *events* will be completed.**

In the original Hebrew it states: **mow`ed** (time), **mow`edim** (times), **chetsiy** (half or middle). Time or **mow`ed** is defined: appointed place, appointed time, meeting, sacred season, set feast, appointed season; appointed sign or signal. -Strong's Concordance.

… a time and times and half a time… 1 + 2+ 1/2 = 3 1/2

In the last half of the seven year tribulation, all Hell will officially break out for…1,260 days = 42 months = time, times, and half a time = 3 1/2 years… Take your pick.

The Apostle Paul tells us the antichrist is taken into custody by Jesus at His second coming.

2 Thessalonians 2:8 Then that lawless one will be revealed whom the Lord will slay with the breath of His mouth and bring to an end by the appearance of His coming…

Signs anyone

With the rapture, there are no signs pointing to the event. With the second coming, there are many signs pointing to the event. Jesus' Olivet Discourse in **Matthew 24** is a chapter dedicated to signs of His second coming.

Jesus tells us there will be false prophets and others claiming to be the Messiah. Jesus warns us in **Matthew 24** with 5 different verses. Beware of false teachers and prophets. We must know what the truth of the matter is or we will be deceived. The lie that is coming is so good, it would deceive believers if possible. This is a serious warning from Jesus Himself.

Matthew 24:5 For many will come in My name, saying, 'I am the Christ,' and will mislead many.

Matthew 24:11 Many false prophets will arise and will mislead many.

Matthew 24:23-26 Then if anyone says to you, 'Behold, here is the Christ,' or 'There He is,' do not believe him. For false Christs and false prophets will arise and will show great signs and wonders, so as to mislead, if possible, even the elect. Behold, I have told you in advance. So if they say to you, 'Behold, He is in the wilderness,' do not go out, or, 'Behold, He is in the inner rooms,' do not believe them.

There are consequences for being deceived and leaning on false teachings and prophets. Our hearts get hardened by God toward the truth.

2 Thessalonians 2:11-12 For this reason God will send upon them a deluding influence so that they will believe what is false, in order that they all may be judged who did not believe the truth, but took pleasure in wickedness.

Conflict will be a hallmark of the day. There will be a drumbeat of violence and war.

Matthew 24:6a You will hear of wars and rumors of wars…

Matthew 24:7a For nation will rise against nation, and kingdom against kingdom…

Humanity will treat their fellow man poorly.

Matthew 24:9-10 Then they will deliver you to tribulation, and will kill you, and you will be hated by all nations because of My name. At that time many will fall away and will betray one another and hate one another.

Matthew 24:12 Because lawlessness is increased, most people's love will grow cold.

Starvation will be a part of the landscape prior to the return of Jesus. Seismic activity will be on the increase.

Matthew 24:7b …and in various places there will be famines and earthquakes.

We are called to look to the heavens.

Matthew 24:29 Immediately after the tribulation of those days the sun will be darkened, and the moon will not give its light, and the stars will fall from heaven, and the powers of the heavens will be shaken.

The antichrist will defile a rebuilt third Jewish Temple.

Matthew 24:15 So when you see the abomination of desolation spoken of by the prophet Daniel, standing in the holy place (let the reader understand)…

Considering Satan

Satan is free to roam before and after the resurrection and the rapture. In fact, he swings into action once the restraint of the Holy Spirit is removed. His first course of action is to empower his minion the antichrist.

2 Thessalonians 2:9-10 *that is,* the one whose coming is in accord with the activity of Satan, with all power and signs and false wonders, and with all the deception of wickedness for those who perish, because they did not receive the love of the truth so as to be saved.

At the second coming, Satan gets a 1,000 year incarceration and time out. Satan is on the chain gang. His imprisonment is the time marker for the beginning of the Millennial Kingdom.

Revelation 20:1-3a Then I saw an angel coming down from heaven, holding the key of the abyss and a great chain in his hand. And he laid hold of the dragon, the serpent of old, who is the devil and Satan, and bound him for a thousand years; and he threw him into the abyss, and shut *it* and sealed *it* over him, so that he would not deceive the nations any longer, until the thousand years were completed...

Who is Involved?

Believers in Jesus Christ participate in the resurrection and rapture. Letters to believers in Thessalonica and Corinth are examples. The Apostle Paul tells of a future event regarding Christ gathering His body or bride. The event is the believer overcoming death in Christ.

It is noted in **1 Thessalonians 4:16-17.**

1 Corinthians 15:52 in a moment, in the twinkling of an eye, at the last trumpet; for the trumpet will sound, and the dead will be raised imperishable, and we will be changed.

Don't sweat it, Jesus has this. There is one condition. You have to believe.

John 14:1-3 "Do not let your heart be troubled; believe in God, believe also in Me. In My Father's house are many dwelling places; if it were not so, I would have told you; for I go to prepare a place for you. If I go and prepare a place for you, I will come again and receive you to Myself, that where I am, there you may be also."

It is a different story and group of people for those involved in the second coming of Christ. Jesus will be returning to the Earth from Heaven with His glorified believers. This promise is from the earliest times of humanity in the person of Enoch.

Jude 1:14 *It was* also about these men *that* Enoch, *in* the seventh *generation* from Adam, prophesied, saying, "Behold, the Lord came with many thousands of His holy ones...

1 Thessalonians 3:13 so that He may establish your hearts without blame in holiness before our God and Father at the coming of our Lord Jesus with all His saints.

The remainder of humanity is involved. Jesus is not returning as the meek and mild Savior. The second time He comes as a Lion. He will be returning as a conquering King. He is going to prevail and He is not in need of assistance.

Isaiah 63:3-6 "I have trodden the wine trough alone, and from the peoples there was no man with Me. I also trod them in My anger and trampled them in My wrath; and their lifeblood is sprinkled on My garments, and I stained all My raiment. For the day of vengeance was in My heart, and My year of redemption has come. I looked, and there was no one to help, and I was astonished and there was no one to uphold; so My own arm brought salvation to Me, and My wrath upheld Me. I trod down the peoples in My anger and made them drunk in My wrath, and I poured out their lifeblood on the earth."

Blessing or Judgment

The second coming of Jesus Christ is the culmination of judgment on Earth. Seven years of Hell on Earth will precede the event. Sooner or later, we are all accountable and meet our Creator. For those who survive, they will meet their maker.

Jude 1:15 to execute judgment upon all, and to convict all the ungodly of all their ungodly deeds which they have done in an ungodly way, and of all the harsh things which ungodly sinners have spoken against Him.

The event of the resurrection and rapture is a blessing. It is our redemption. It is where we exchange our current body of sin for an eternal, glorified body. Death has been overcome through Christ.

1 Corinthians 15:54 When the perishable puts on the imperishable, and the mortal puts on immortality, then shall come to pass the saying that is written: "Death is swallowed up in victory."

1 Corinthians 15:57 But thanks be to God, who gives us the victory through our Lord Jesus Christ!

1 Thessalonians 4:18 Therefore comfort one another with these words.

1 Thessalonians 5:11 Therefore encourage one another and build up one another, just as you also are doing.

Our lives end in judgment one way or another. We are accountable for what we think, say, and do in this life. We can choose to have Jesus take our place of judgment by His crosswork. Or we can ignore His offer and stand before God on our own two feet. Choose wisely…

Chapter 7

Time, Time, Time

1 Corinthians 15:51-52 Behold, I tell you a mystery; we will not all sleep, but we will all be changed, in a moment, in the twinkling of an eye, at the last trumpet; for the trumpet will sound, and the dead will be raised imperishable, and we will be changed.

…at the last trumpet…

There is a lot of discussion and debate regarding this phrase. What is the reference? Let's go back to Moses and the book of **Leviticus**.

Leviticus 23:23-25 Again the LORD spoke to Moses, saying, "Speak to the sons of Israel, saying, 'In the seventh month on the first of the month you shall have a rest, a reminder by blowing *of trumpets,* a holy convocation. 'You shall not do any laborious work, but you shall present an offering by fire to the LORD.'"

This appointment is also referenced in **Numbers 29:1 On the first day of the seventh month, you are to hold a holy assembly. You must not do your ordinary work, for it is a day of blowing trumpets for you.**

God's first fall appointment has many names. It is called the Feast of Trumpets by Christians. It is recognized as the Jewish New Year, Rosh Hashanah, or the head of years. Some refer to it as the "Hidden Day" or the "Wedding of the Messiah". In Judaism, it is called Yom Teruah which means the "Day of Blowing". Some call it the New Moon Festival. These terms are synonymous.

It is the beginning of the Jewish civil new year. The date for Yom Teruah is (traditional Hebrew calendar) depending on the sighting of the new moon. The new year begins when the new moon is confirmed by two witnesses. Yom Teruah is officially declared when the crescent of the new moon is observed by two witness and confirmed by the high priest. By definition, it is a holiday **no one knows the day or hour.**

God operates on a lunar calendar. Jews have utilized the following procedure every month for thousands of years. It is called **Rosh Chodesh** which means "head of the month". At the end of a lunar cycle, the moon is dark and is not seen for 2-3 days. So, the new moon could be identified during this 2-3 day period **...of that day or hour no one knows...**

There are people who are trained witnesses to identify the new moon. They are outside of Jerusalem when the moon goes dark and they are looking for the tiny sliver to emerge. If you are interested, see this website link.

http://whenisthenewmoon.com/

Yom Teruah means the "Day of Blowing". And blow the trumpets they do.

The directions for the holiday are straight forward. 1) It is to be a day of rest or a Sabbath. 2) The day is a holy or separate day. It is a convocation. The Hebrew word for "convocation" is **miqra'**. Per Strong's Concordance it means: rehearsal, convocation, a reading, a calling together, or sacred assembly. 3) It is a memorial and reminder to blow or shout.

The Hebrew word is **teruah.** It means: alarm, signal, a sound of tempest, shout of joy, blast of war, alarm, joy, war-cry, or battle-cry. -Strong's Concordance

Judaism recognizes three trumps: first trump, the last trump, and the great trump. Each one of these named trumps represents a specific day.

The "first trump" is blown on the Feast of Pentecost. **Exodus 19:19 When the sound of the trumpet grew louder and louder, Moses spoke and God answered him with thunder.**

The "great trump" is blown on Yom Kippur and signals the return of Christ to Earth. **Matthew 24:31 And he will send out his angels with a loud trumpet call, and they will gather his elect from the four winds, from one end of heaven to the other.**

The "last trump" is synonymous with Yom Teruah or Rosh Hashanah. **1 Corinthians 15:52 …in a moment, in the twinkling of an eye, at the last trumpet; for the trumpet will sound, and the dead will be raised imperishable, and we will be changed.**

Resources: Festivals of the Jewish Year, Theodore Gaster; The High Holy Days, Herman Kieval.

Jews have rehearsed and celebrated this holiday every year for thousands of years. The Hebrew grammar suggests this is a dress rehearsal for an appointed date and time. The holiday consists of a pattern of shofar or ram's horn blasts. There are three different sounds. Each is blown three times for a total of 9 blasts. This pattern is completed 11 times for a total of 99 blasts. The last blast is set aside. It is the longest and loudest. It is known as the "Last Trump".

References provided by: www.jewfaq.org, www.chabad.org, www.myjewishlearning.com, El Shaddai Ministries.

No one knows the day or hour…

Matthew 24:36 But of that day and hour no one knows, not even the angels of heaven, nor the Son, but the Father alone. -Jesus

Jesus is talking to His disciples about the end of the age and His second coming. In our western culture, we take this passage literally. "Nobody knows, not even Jesus, Jesus said!" Okay, we are done here, moving forward.

Wait a minute, Jesus is a Jew. Matthew, the author, is a Jew. Culturally, the Bible is a Jewish book. It is not to be viewed from a western culture perspective. The Apostle Paul, the ultimate academic Jew, tells us in **1 Corinthians 15,** the resurrection of the dead in Christ is associated with the rapture of believers in Jesus. The verse below is also quoted by Mark, who is a Jew.

Mark 13:32 But of that day or hour no one knows, not even the angels in heaven, nor the Son, but the Father *alone.*

By way of review, there is only one Jewish Holiday by definition, **of that day or hour no one knows.** Because, this day is a new moon holiday. Of all the God appointed holidays, this is the only holiday occurring on a new moon. The holiday has many names. Again, it is the Jewish New Year, Rosh Hashanah. Jews call it Yom Teruah (literally means "day of blowing" in Hebrew). It is referred to as the "Hidden Day" in Jewish culture. It is called the Day of Judgment. Christians call it the Feast of Trumpets.

According to Jewish tradition the purpose of the trumpet blasts is to awaken the dead, resurrection.

Remember how a new moon or a new month is determined? God operates on a lunar calendar. Jews have utilized the following procedure every month for thousands of years. It is called **Rosh Chodesh** which means "head of the month". At the end of a lunar cycle, the moon is dark and is not seen for 2-3 days. So, the new moon could be identified during this 2-3 day period …**of that day or hour no one knows…**By definition, a new moon is proclaimed when the first little sliver emerges from a darkened moon. It is a tiny crescent that is noted briefly at sunset on the western horizon. The month begins at the sighting of the new moon. Two witnesses have to confirm the sighting. Upon agreement, the two witnesses report to the high priest.

Who is our high priest? Jesus.

Hebrews 2:17 Therefore, He had to be made like His brethren in all things, so that He might become a merciful and faithful high priest in things pertaining to God, to make propitiation for the sins of the people.

Hebrews 3:1 Therefore, holy brethren, partakers of a heavenly calling, consider Jesus, the Apostle and High Priest of our confession…

Hebrews 4:14 Therefore, since we have a great high priest who has passed through the heavens, Jesus the Son of God, let us hold fast our confession.

What is the role of the high priest? The role of the high priest is to intercede to God on behalf of the people. Only the Father knows the day or the hour to confirm the new moon. When the new moon is confirmed, the trumpet (shofar or ram's horn) is blown.

Notice, this language is also consistent with ancient Jewish wedding customs. The father sends the son or groom to get his bride. Only the father knows the day or the hour of the wedding.

Yom Teruah is the new moon holiday. Rosh Hashanah is the only Jewish holiday that falls on the first day of a month. The Feast of Trumpets is the only new moon holiday. **But of that day and hour no one knows…**It is a "Hidden Day". Investigate, think about it.

Jewish cultural customs provided by: www.torahcalendar.com, Festivals of the Jewish Year by Theodore Gaster, The High Holy Days by Herman Kieval, El Shaddai Ministries, The New Manners and Customs of Bible Times, God's Final Jubilee by Dan Goodwin, Our Father Abraham Jewish Roots of the Christian Faith by Marvin R. Wilson.

I tell you a mystery…

1 Corinthians 15:51-52 Behold, I tell you a mystery; we will not all sleep, but we will all be changed, in a moment, in the twinkling of an eye, at the last trumpet; for the trumpet will sound, and the dead will be raised imperishable, and we will be changed.

There are many cultural bridges to cross in these two verses. The New Testament is written in Greek. But the New Testament is still culturally Jewish. Paul was a trained Jew of the highest order. He had the best Jewish education going. He grew up in Jerusalem and studied under the famous teacher Gamaliel (**Acts 22:3**) and he was a member of the Pharisees (**Philippians 3:5**). Paul's father was a member of the Pharisees (**Acts 23:6**). Paul is the author of **1 Corinthians** and several other New Testament epistles.

In western culture, a mystery is defined as something that is difficult or impossible to understand or explain.

In the Greek language, the word for "mystery" is **μυστεριον/musterion.** It means: of God; the secret counsels which govern God in dealing with the righteous, which are hidden from ungodly and wicked men but plain to the godly. -Strong's Concordance

In other words, it is information revealed that was not previously known.

In the New Testament it denotes, not the mysterious (as with the English word), but that which, being outside the range of unassisted natural apprehension, can be made known only by Divine revelation, and is made known in a manner and at a time appointed by God, and to those only who are illumined by His Spirit. In the ordinary sense a "mystery" implies knowledge withheld; its Scriptural significance is truth revealed. Hence the terms especially associated with the subject are: made known, manifested, revealed, preached, understood, and of dispensation. -Vine's Expository Dictionary of New Testament Words

The definition given for "mystery" may be best illustrated by the following passage.

Colossians 1:26 the mystery that has been kept hidden for ages and generations, but is now disclosed to the saints.

The Apostle Paul is going to teach and explain new information.

1 Corinthians 15:51-52 Behold, I tell you a mystery; we will not all sleep, but we will all be changed, in a moment, in the twinkling of an eye, at the last trumpet; for the trumpet will sound, and the dead will be raised imperishable, and we will be changed.

"Sleep" is an idiom for those who have died. These are the dead in Christ. They are not taking an afternoon nap or slumbering at night. **...but we will all be changed...** "All" would include the dead and those alive at the time of this event in Christ.

The million dollar question, when is this going to happen? This is where things get real interesting.

...in a moment... In the Greek, the word is **ατομοσ/atomos.** We get our English word atom from this. Per Strong's Concordance it means: that cannot be cut in two, or divided, indivisible, of a moment of time.

The change to our eternal body happens so quickly, one cannot divide that moment of time.

…in the twinkling of any eye… In the Greek, the word for "twinkling" is **ρηιπε/rhipe.** Per Strong's Concordance it means: throw, stroke, beat, a moment of time. The blinking of an eye.

With these two definitions, there is emphasis of the speed of transition to an eternal body of those in Christ. When this event occurs, it will be essentially instantaneous. In our western culture, we take this literally and look no further.

But, to the Jew…**in the twinkling of any eye…**It is a time point, it is twilight. This is when darkness is officially declared.

www.torahcalendar.com/SUNSET.asp

Is the Apostle Paul communicating a time point?

Colossians 2:16-17 Therefore no one is to act as your judge in regard to food or drink or in respect to a festival or a new moon or a Sabbath day— things which are a *mere* shadow of what is to come; but the substance belongs to Christ.

"Judge" or **krinos** in the Greek: The action of the verb is continuous.

Meaning of **κρινο/krinos**: to approve, esteem, to prefer; to be of opinion, deem, think; to determine, resolve, decree; to go to law, have suit at law. -Strong's Concordance

Do not let any one pass judgment or censure continuously. It is not any one's place to scoff or mock the practice of God's appointed holidays. The food of the festival include round challah bread, apples dipped in honey, and pomegranates.

Apples are dipped in honey and eaten for the promise of a "sweet year".

Tradition has a round challah bread for the Lord as King.

Jews symbolically throw their sins into the river or a body of water. They rid themselves of sin.

www.hebrew4christians.com/Holidays/Fall_Holidays/Rosh_Hashan nah/rosh_hashannah.html

Numbers 29:1 and **Leviticus 23:23-25** state the appointment is a Sabbath Day of rest...**you shall do no laborious work.** The holiday is an appointed day off. So be ready!

The Apostle Paul states these elements **are a *mere* shadow of what is to come.** The Greek word for "shadow" is **σκια/skia**. It means: an image cast by an object and representing the form of that object.

The Feast of Trumpets is a shadow cast by Jesus Christ. God has appointed this holiday as a day of prophetic significance. I take it Jesus has **BIG PLANS** for this holiday at some point in the future.

...the substance belongs to Christ.

Toward who do we cast our sins? **Micah 7:19 He will again have compassion on us; he will tread our iniquities underfoot. You will cast all our sins into the depths of the sea.**

Who is our King? As believers, we will rule and reign with Him in the Kingdom to come (**Revelation 1:6, 3:21, 20:4, 20:6, 2 Timothy 2:12**).

We are baptized in Christ as believers (**Galatians 3:27, Colossians 2:12, Romans 6:3**).

There are seven God appointed holidays communicated through the Old Testament Law. Does the information God communicated to Moses on Mount Sinai thousands of years ago really matter to us today and beyond? The first four appointments were fulfilled to the day by Jesus Himself with His death, burial, resurrection, and the giving of the Holy Spirit. If the first four spring holidays were fulfilled on the God appointed holiday, why would the fall holidays be any different?

The Hebrew people have been practicing the appointment every year for approximately 3,500 years on the first day of the seventh month per the Mosaic Law. This is not some Old Testament warm and fuzzy tradition. God has a point and a reason. He has not forgotten. The Feast of Trumpets is the only new moon holiday on God's calendar. Yom Teruah is set aside by God with prophetic implications. The Feast of Trumpets is a promise for the future.

Has the Apostle Paul connected the dots?

1 Corinthians 15:52 in a moment, in the twinkling of an eye, at the last trumpet; for the trumpet will sound, and the dead will be raised imperishable, and we will be changed.

1 Thessalonians 4:16-17 For the Lord Himself will descend from heaven with a shout, with the voice of *the* archangel and with the trumpet of God, and the dead in Christ will rise first. Then we who are alive and remain will be caught up together with them in the clouds to meet the Lord in the air, and so we shall always be with the Lord.

Resurrection and rapture on the Feast of Trumpets??? Resurrection and rapture, Jesus Christ makes it happen. The issue may not be the hour or the day. The issue may be the year…

Chapter 8
Raptures in the Old Testament

This chapter of the book is going to focus on examples of rapture events in the Old Testament. Enoch was taken by God approximately 3,000 years before Jesus Christ. David wrote the book of Psalms roughly 1,000 years before Jesus. Elijah's rapture event in the chariot of fire was roughly 800 years until the time of Jesus. Isaiah wrote his prophecies about 700 years before the birth of Christ. Zephaniah wrote his prophecies approximately 630 years before Jesus Christ. Across the span of five authors and thousands of years, the message is consistent. Rapture occurs before judgement. All of these Old Testament examples below will demonstrate this pattern. Dates provided by Nelson Complete Book of Bible Maps & Charts.

Enoch

To the critic who says, "There is no such thing as a 'rapture'." Sorry, that is incorrect. For the very first 'rapture', go all the way back to the **Book of Genesis**. This event takes place **before** the flood of Noah.

Genesis 5:21-24 Enoch lived sixty-five years, and became the father of Methuselah. Then Enoch walked with God three hundred years after he became the father of Methuselah, and he had *other* sons and daughters. So all the days of Enoch were three hundred and sixty-five years. Enoch walked with God; and he was not, for God took him.

Becoming a father clearly resulted in a changed attitude for Enoch. At that point, the Hebrew grammar suggests Enoch responded to God and **"walked with Him"**. The name Enoch means "dedicate" per Strong's Concordance. Enoch dedicated himself to God. Jewish tradition states Enoch was a preacher.

The meaning of the name of Methuselah is a bit of a mystery. Here are a couple of possibilities. One is "man of the dart" per Strong's

Concordance. A second is "when he is dead it shall be sent" per Jones' Dictionary of Old Testament Proper Names. The issue is the root of the name. Is it "mut" (death) or "mat" (man) in the original Hebrew?

Did Enoch know judgment was coming from God? Something caused Enoch to rethink his attitude. The ages of the people documented in Genesis as time points would suggest the flood began when Methuselah died. Methuselah lived the longest of any man, 969 years (**Genesis 5:27**). God allowed the greatest amount of time for humanity to repent of their actions before judgment came. But, when the time came He acted swiftly and decisively with a global flood.

Note, Enoch was not around during the course of the flood. He was taken off of the earth before the world wide judgment of God came. He was spared and did not have to go through the global tribulation of that time.

...for God took him. The meaning of "took" in Hebrew is "**laqach**". Strong's Concordance defines the word as: to take, take in the hand, carry along, carry away, take away, or to fetch.

Another definition is to take to or for a person, procure, get, take possession of, select, choose, take in marriage, receive, or accept. The concept of taking in marriage is noted in the Hebrew Old Testament word "**laqach**" and the Greek New Testament word "**harpazo**". Language of a marriage is noted with Christ and His bride the Church throughout the New Testament. Terms for rapture in the Old Testament and the New Testament center around the concept of marriage and a groom taking or snatching his bride.

Enoch was not a Jew or citizen of the country Israel. Nations were not in existence before the flood. Is Enoch a type or foreshadowing of the rapture of the bride of Christ, the church? Is there a group of people who will be taken away before a worldwide judgment of God in the tribulation? Enoch was removed before the global flood. There is a precedent.

Some may say Enoch is just an Old Testament story and fable. The story of **Genesis** is confirmed by the author of **Hebrews**.

Hebrews 11:5 By faith Enoch was taken up so that he would not see death; AND HE WAS NOT FOUND BECAUSE GOD TOOK HIM UP; for he obtained the witness that before his being taken up he was pleasing to God.

Enoch did not taste death. He was taken off of the Earth prior to the global judgment and flood.

Hebrews 11:6 And without faith it is impossible to please *Him,* for he who comes to God must believe that He is and *that* He is a rewarder of those who seek Him.

Elijah

Elijah is an interesting story. Scripture tells us he is from Tishbe in Gilead. **1 Kings 17:1a Now Elijah the Tishbite, who was of the settlers of Gilead...**The exact location of Tishbe is unknown. It is thought to be southeast of the Sea of Galilee on the Brook Cherith. That is about all we know of Elijah's origins. His family is not mentioned. There is no genealogy for Elijah. Scholars conjecture he may not have been an Israelite because he was born in the region of Gilead near Ammon. This region would be modern day Jordan (Nelson's Complete Book of Bible Maps, p. 118).

In the Hebrew, Elijah means "my God is Jehovah".

2 Kings 2:11 As they were going along and talking, behold, *there appeared* a chariot of fire and horses of fire which separated the two of them. And Elijah went up by a whirlwind to heaven.

Elisha was not the only witness to this event. **2 Kings 2:7 Now fifty men of the sons of the prophets went and stood opposite *them* at a distance, while the two of them stood by the Jordan.** The text says there were at least 51 others at the event site.

Elijah and Elisha knew God was coming to get Elijah. This is documented and noted frequently in **2 Kings 2:1-11.** Members of the prophetic guild or school in Bethel knew Elijah's rapture was coming.

2 Kings 2:3 Then the sons of the prophets who *were at* Bethel came out to Elisha and said to him, "Do you know that the Lord

will take away your master from over you today?" And he said, "Yes, I know; be still."

People in Jericho were aware of Elijah's pending rapture. They were aware that God was coming to take Elijah. They told Elisha all about it.

2 Kings 2:5 The sons of the prophets who *were* at Jericho approached Elisha and said to him, "Do you know that the Lord will take away your master from over you today?" And he answered, "Yes, I know; be still."

Hundreds of people knew Elijah was going to be taken into Heaven. As history would show, Elijah was taken away before the fall of Israel and Judah. Elijah was raptured before judgment on Israel and Judah. A second example of a believer who was spared from God's pending judgment.

Things are no different today. There has been notification for over 1,900 years. People are aware there is a time coming when those who believe in Christ will be taken into the clouds to meet the Lord.

1 Thessalonians 4:17 Then we who are alive and remain will be caught up together with them in the clouds to meet the Lord in the air, and so we shall always be with the Lord.

Elijah's resume: Rapture, return, death, resurrection, and ascension…That is quite an experience through time that will span over 2,700 linear years.

Rapture in Isaiah 57

John 14:2-3 "In My Father's house are many dwelling places; if it were not so, I would have told you; for I go to prepare a place for you. If I go and prepare a place for you, I will come again and receive you to Myself, that where I am, *there* you may be also."

In this passage, Jesus is talking with His disciples. Some translate "dwelling places" as "mansions". Bottom line, Jesus is building a really nice place in Heaven. We know where He is now in the 21st century. He is at the right hand of the Father in Heaven.

Mark 16:19 After the Lord Jesus had spoken to them, he was taken up into heaven and sat down at the right hand of God.

Acts 2:33a Therefore having been exalted to the right hand of God…

1 Peter 3:22 who is at the right hand of God, having gone into heaven, after angels and authorities and powers had been subjected to Him.

Then He states He will come again to get others. Since He is in Heaven, He will return to "receive" or παραλαμβανο/paralambano (original Greek word). Per Strong's Concordance, it means: to take or join with one's self. The grammar indicates this is a future event that is certain to happen. He will certainly take people to join Him in Heaven. Note, there is no mention of His physical return to Earth. This is an event where He gathers people to meet Him in Heaven.

Now why would Jesus take people away from Earth? What purpose does that serve? The Old Testament has answers…

Isaiah 57:1-2 The righteous man perishes, and no man takes it to heart; and devout men are taken away, while no one understands. For the righteous man is taken away from evil, He enters into peace; they rest in their beds, e*ach one* who walked in his upright way.

The righteous man perishes, and no man takes it to heart… A just and lawful man dies or **'abad** in the original Hebrew. The word **'abad** can also mean perish, exterminated, or destroyed per Strong's Concordance. The response from the culture, "Who cares".

…and devout men are taken away, while no one understands…These men are taken away or **'acaph** in the original Hebrew. The word **'acaph** can also mean: collect, to gather (an individual into company of others), to bring up the rear, to gather and take away, remove, withdraw. These men did not die. They have been gathered into a group and taken away. They are withdrawn and removed from bad and evil. The response from the culture is a lack of understanding or discernment. The culture is clueless. "What just happened? Where did they go?"

For the righteous man is taken away from evil, he enters into peace… God's people, dead or alive, are removed from bad and evil. Their destination is "**shalom**" not "**sheol**" or the grave, which is the place for the dead. **Shalom** is the Hebrew word for peace. Strong's Concordance defines **shalom** as: completeness, soundness, welfare, peace, safety, health, prosperity, quiet, tranquility, contentment, friendship of human relationships, and friendship with God especially in covenant relationship.

A group of just people are removed from an awful situation. They enter into a place of safety and tranquility.

This stuff is in the Old Testament! It has always been there. It is consistent with the message in the New Testament.

1 Thessalonians 5:9-10 For God has not destined us for wrath, but for obtaining salvation through our Lord Jesus Christ, who died for us, so that whether we are awake or asleep, we will live together with Him.

Rapture in Psalm 27

Psalm 27:5 For in the day of trouble He will conceal me in His tabernacle; in the secret place of His tent He will hide me; He will lift me up on a rock.

The context of **Psalm 27** is trusting in God. Trust in God even when life looks really bleak and desperate. David was surrounded by enemies. He called on God to protect and deliver him from his situation.

For in the day of trouble He will conceal me in His tabernacle…The language in the Hebrew is definitive. God will certainly do it. He will carefully hide me in His home.

This will occur in the day of "trouble" or **ra`** in the Hebrew. **Ra`** is the Hebrew word that is opposed to good. Simply stated, it is a bad or evil time.

…in the secret place of His tent He will hide me…The text states twice in the verse, God will selectively hide. He is the source of action. His dwelling is sacred.

He will lift me up on a rock. The original text states God will raise or elevate one up to a rock, cliff, or rocky wall. The bottom line, nobody is going to get you. This is a very safe place. It is God's home and it cannot be penetrated by wickedness. He has carefully placed one in His fortified shelter.

Three times it is stated in **Psalm 27:5**. **He will** do all the heavy lifting.

The pattern is intact. Removal and safety before trouble comes. Kick back, relax. God has this one.

Rapture in Isaiah 26

Isaiah 26:19 Your dead will live; their corpses will rise. You who lie in the dust, awake and shout for joy, for your dew *is as* the dew of the dawn, and the earth will give birth to the departed spirits.

The text makes it very clear. These people are dead. The Hebrew word for dead in this case is **muwth**. It means to die (as a penalty), to be put to death, or to die prematurely (by neglect of wise moral conduct). -Strong's Concordance

Humanity was originally created to be eternal. We are reminded death is a result of sinful choices. The body is a corpse, a carcass. The executed are buried and taking a dirt nap.

But as the pattern of Scripture, the dead are called and commanded. The Hebrew grammar states these dead bodies are caused to wake up. Something, God, has acted on the dead bodies to cause them to awaken. Their response to being resurrected is an intensive, crying yell for joy according to the original grammar. This seems to be a plausible response if you had been dead for years.

Again, the text confirms the original point. These people were dead. The Hebrew word for departed spirits is **rapha'**. Per Strong's Concordance, **rapha'** means spirit or ghost of the dead. Body and spirit have been reunited.

There are cultural implications regarding dust to the Jew. God created from Adam from dust. Adam returned to the dust as a result of sin/death.

Genesis 3:19 "By the sweat of your face You will eat bread, till you return to the ground, because from it you were taken; for you are dust, and to dust you shall return."

Dust is associated with death.

Psalm 22:15b…And You lay me in the dust of death.

Dust is the fate of humans and animals as noted in **Ecclesiastes 3:20 Both go to the same place, both come from the dust, and to dust both return.**

Whereas dust is associated with death, dew is associated with life. Dew is a symbol of fertility and life (NET Bible). The context of the verses is nation Israel and their dead. This verse says Israel's dead will be a symbol of life and rebirth to the world. After approximately 2,000 years of being exiled from their land and dead as a nation, this has literally come to pass. In 1948, Israel became a nation again, a resurrected country. See **Ezekiel 37,** the valley of dry bones, for more detail. In the future, there will be multiple resurrections of the dead.

The resurrection of Jesus demonstrates mastery over death and sin.

Isaiah 25:18 He will swallow up death for all time, and the Lord GOD will wipe tears away from all faces, and He will remove the reproach of His people from all the earth; for the LORD has spoken.

The context of these verses in **Isaiah** has the resurrection first and then there is this…

Isaiah 26:20 Come, my people, enter into your rooms and close your doors behind you; hide for a little while until indignation runs *its* course.

God's people are invited. Come on in! This is your room and shut the door. The room is in the inner most chamber per the Hebrew vocabulary.

…hide for a little while…The idea in the Hebrew with the word "hide" is **chabah**. It means to conceal oneself, remain hidden, or withdraw. It is not forever but only a small, little time.

…until indignation runs *its* course. Indignation is **za`am** in the Hebrew. It is also translated anger. The fury and wrath will come to pass. -Strong's Concordance.

Those who believe in God are being invited to a hiding place that God has made for them. The reason is to avoid God's wrath or anger. God is protecting His people from judgment. This statement is made by the prophet Isaiah 700 years before the birth of Jesus Christ. This is not out of the New Testament and the Apostle Paul.

Isaiah 26:21 For behold, the Lord is about to come out from His place to punish the inhabitants of the earth for their iniquity; and the earth will reveal her bloodshed and will no longer cover her slain.

For behold, the Lord is about to come out from His place…We know God's abode is Heaven. Heads up, He is leaving His station. His people are hidden safely away. Now why would he do a thing like that?

…to punish the inhabitants of the earth for their iniquity…The Hebrew word for "punish" is **paqad**. There is more to this word than "punish". Strong's Concordance defines **paqad** as: to pay attention to, observe; to attend to; to seek, look about for; to seek in vain, need, miss, lack; to visit upon, punish; to pass in review, muster, number; to appoint, assign, lay upon as a charge, deposit.

Attention sinners of Earth! Those of you who are left behind. There will be no stone unturned. The Lord is actively looking for every, single transgression with every intent of finding sin. He is absolutely focused on prosecution.

…and the earth will reveal her bloodshed and will no longer cover her slain.

The earth or the land "will reveal" or **galah** in the Hebrew. The term could also be translated as: to uncover nakedness; to disclose, discover or lay bare; to make known, show, or reveal.

The earth "will no longer cover" or **kacah**. This word could be defined as: clothe; to cover or conceal; to cover (for protection); to spread over. -Strong's Concordance

God makes the point twice in this verse as an emphasis. The land will expose itself of its bloodshed, violence, and murder. The cover ups are going to end. In the final analysis, humanity's violence toward their fellow man will all come to light.

There is a word for this concept in the New Testament...**Apocalypse**.

God chose to unveil or **apokalupsis/ αποκαλυπσισ** in the Greek. It means to literally "take the cover off". The word could be further defined as: laying bear, making naked; a disclosure of truth, instruction; concerning things before unknown; things withdrawn from view are made visible to all; manifestation, appearance. -Strong's Concordance

God is exposing the naked truth as He uncovers sin in judgment in the book of **Revelation**.

Rapture in Zephaniah 2

Zephaniah 2:2-3 Before the decree takes effect. The day passes like the chaff. Before the burning anger of the Lord comes upon you, before the day of the Lord's anger comes upon you.

Seek the Lord, all you humble of the earth who have carried out His ordinances; seek righteousness, seek humility. Perhaps you will be hidden in the day of the Lord's anger.

The Lord is talking. Specifically, His name is **YHWH**.

YHWH (scholars refer to this as the Tetragrammaton, Greek for four letters) is the proper name of the Hebrew God of the Bible. The correct spelling is **YHWH**. Note there are no vowels in this term. Vowels from the name Adonai were substituted and the term Yahweh emerged. Jehovah is a word that has been translated to English from the Hebrew, Yahweh. The name for LORD is Jehovah. It means the existing one. This name is so sacred, Jews refuse to pronounce it. The name is first introduced in **Exodus 3:14** when

Moses and God are having a discussion. His name is a statement of being.

Exodus 3:14 God said to Moses, "I AM WHO I AM"; and He said, "Thus you shall say to the sons of Israel, 'I AM has sent me to you.'"

The Lord, Yahweh is discussing a time point. He makes His case crystal clear. **Before, Before, Before...** Three times He makes the point. One, **Before the decree...**Two, **Before the burning anger...**Three, **before the day of the Lord's anger...**

Before the decree takes effect. The Hebrew term for "decree" is **choq.** This is a legal term. "Decree" could also be defined as a statute or ordinance. A law or rule will be definitively judged at some point in time.

But **before,** there will be an `**abar.**` This is an opportunity "to pass through" and avoid the **Lord's anger.** In these verses in **Zephaniah 2**, this is the first mention of avoiding God's judgment.

There needs to be some reflection and a changing of the mind. God tells us what is coming, His anger. He states three times in the two verses; anger is coming and there will be execution of justice.

`aph is the Hebrew word for "angry". This is not your garden variety angry. It is extreme and furious wrath.

God is not an overbearing ogre who wants to crush us with His thumb because of our short comings. He gives instructions and a way of deliverance from His wrath. He is merciful, gracious, and forgiving.

Three times He tells us to "seek". The Hebrew grammar says we are to "seek" purposefully and intentionally with intensity. The idea is more than looking. It even involves asking or requesting. Secure, face, desire, or demand are the ideas.

The first thing we "seek" is the Lord. We know who the great "I Am" is. He is none other than Jesus Christ. He has taken our wrath and judgment at the cross. His death and shed blood have satisfied the legal payment of the decree. The penalty has been paid.

There are expectations in character. He expects us to behave and **carry out His ordinances**. Out of gratitude, we should "seek" to do what is right. We should "seek" humility because we would otherwise be found guilty and judged.

The character traits we seek are Christ-like; obedient to doing things right and humility (**Philippians 2**).

2 Corinthians 5:21 He made Him who knew no sin *to be* sin on our behalf, so that we might become the righteousness of God in Him.

Why does all of this matter? **Perhaps you will be hidden in the day of the Lord's anger.**

There will be some who are **cathar** in the Hebrew. They will be carefully concealed and hidden. And when will they be concealed???…**in the day of the Lord's anger.**

And that my friends are concrete examples of a pre tribulation rapture in the Old Testament.

Chapter 9

The Kinsman Redeemer

Jesus Christ, Kinsman Redeemer

The Hebrew word for "redeemer" is **ga'al**. A kinsman redeemer will pay off one's debts, defend the family, avenge a killing, and marry the widow of the deceased (definition of kinsman redeemer provided by NET Bible).

The first mention of the kinsman redeemer concept is in **Genesis**. Jacob is on his death bed and he is about to give prophetic blessing to his sons. The context is the blessing of his son Joseph. Joseph was the first to be blessed.

Genesis 48:16 The angel who has <u>redeemed</u> me from all evil, bless the lads; and may my name live on in them, and the names of my fathers Abraham and Isaac; and may they grow into a multitude in the midst of the earth.

Jacob or Israel recognized the angel of the Lord as his redeemer or **ga`al**.

The concept of the kinsman redeemer is noted in arguably the oldest book of the Bible, **Job**.

Job is aware of the concept of resurrection and being brought back to life. He is pleading with God. Will I live again? Job expresses awareness of his bodily change to come. Job knows that God will call before this change.

Job 19:25-27a "As for me, I know that my <u>Redeemer</u> lives, and at the last He will take His stand on the earth. Even after my skin is destroyed, yet from my flesh I shall see God; whom I myself shall behold, and whom my eyes will see and not another. My heart faints within me!"

Job knows his debt for sin will be taken care of. Job knows his Redeemer will avenge the killing of his family members and defend him. Job knows he is going to physically die.

Job 42:17 And Job died, an old man and full of days.

But, he knows he will be resurrected to see his Redeemer with his restored body. His flesh and his eyes will be renewed. The Redeemer lives. This verse reveals the timing of the resurrection...**at the last**.

Job recognizes God as his **ga`al** or redeemer.

Ga`al is the Hebrew word used in the Book of Ruth of Boaz who is the kinsman redeemer. Boaz is a pattern or type for Jesus Christ. The custom of the kinsman redeemer is played out in **Ruth 4.**

There are two conditions for Boaz or any kinsman redeemer to meet. The land of the relative has to be purchased or redeemed and the bride of the deceased relative must be acquired if the deceased was married. In this case, Elimelech (meaning "My God is King" per Strong's Concordance) was the deceased relative. The legal transaction was made in front of ten city elders. Another relative of Elimelech was on board with land acquisition. But he was not interested in acquiring Ruth, the gentile Moabite. Boaz stepped in and exercised his full right as a kinsman redeemer. Boaz purchased the land and acquired Ruth.

The legal contract was a sandal. Witnesses were present and confirmed the transaction.

Ruth 4:7 Now this was *the custom* in former times in Israel concerning the <u>redemption</u> and the exchange *of land* to confirm any matter: a man removed his sandal and gave it to another; and this was the *manner of* attestation in Israel.

It is from this prophetic transaction, blessing would come to Israel and the world. Over 1,000 years later, a Savior would be born in Ephrathah, the area in and around Bethlehem.

Ruth 4:11 All the people who were in the court, and the elders, said, "*We are* witnesses. May the Lord make the woman who is coming into your home like Rachel and Leah, both of whom built the house of Israel; and may you achieve wealth in Ephrathah and become famous in Bethlehem.

The scene in Heaven (**Revelation 5**) is consistent with the customs of a kinsman redeemer (**Ruth 4**). Both are conducted before the court and elders as witnesses before God. With His death Jesus purchased humanity, His bride, from the bondage of sin. He has access to the scroll. The land for redemption is the Earth. Christ is sinless and innocent.

Revelation 5:9-10 And they sang a new song, saying, "Worthy are You to take the book and to break its seals; for You were slain, and <u>purchased</u> for God with Your blood *men* from every tribe and tongue and people and nation. You have made them *to be* a kingdom and priests to our God; and they will reign upon the earth."

Who is our kinsman redeemer? Jesus. We are dead to this world and dead to sin. Christ will marry His bride the church.

Galatians 4:4-5 But when the fullness of the time came, God sent forth His Son, born of a woman, born under the Law, so that He might <u>redeem</u> those who were under the Law, that we might receive the adoption as sons.

The wedding of the kinsman redeemer, Jesus Christ, the groom to his bride the church takes place in Heaven.

Revelation 19:7-8 "Let us rejoice and be glad and give the glory to Him, for the marriage of the Lamb has come and His bride has made herself ready." It was given to her to clothe herself in fine linen, bright and clean; for the fine linen is the righteous acts of the saints.

Chapter 10
The Wedding Ceremony

A Jewish wedding is a classic example of what we as westerners are missing when we read the Bible. Most of us, present company included, do not get Jewish cultural customs. Personally, as the cultural veil has lifted, Jesus makes even more sense. If one understands the order and purpose of a Jewish wedding, then we know the order and sequence of history. A pre tribulation rapture makes perfect sense in the sequence of events.

When looking at the course of an Ancient Jewish wedding, Jesus is following cultural custom. We know who the bride of Christ is. It is the church or the body of believers in Jesus. He has taken, is taking, and will continue to take the necessary steps to marry His bride. Yeshua is fulfilling His prophetic duty as a prospective groom.

Ephesians 5:22-33 Draws parallels between Christ as husband and the church as the bride or wife. Jesus' relationship to the church is as a husband to a wife.

Ephesians 5:32 This mystery is great; but I am speaking with reference to Christ and the church.

Shiddukhin

The first step in the order of marriage events is called the **Shiddukhin**. The groom's Father or his representative chooses a bride for his son. An example of this in the Bible would be **Genesis 24:2-4.**

http://free.messianicbible.com/feature/ancient-jewish-wedding-customs-and-yeshuas-second-coming/

Genesis 24:2-4 Abraham said to his servant, the oldest of his household, who had charge of all that he owned, "Please place your hand under my thigh, and I will make you swear by the Lord, the God of heaven and the God of earth, that you shall not take a wife for my son from the daughters of the Canaanites,

among whom I live, but you will go to my country and to my relatives, and take a wife for my son Isaac."

Think about the oath taken in **verse 2**. There is no way one would forget their pledge or forget their requested purpose. Would you forget a promise made to a man who requested you grab his manhood and swear to God? I think not!

The taking of this oath had to do with the sanctity of the family and the continuation of the family line. D. R. Freedman, "Put Your Hand Under My Thigh - the Patriarchal Oath," *BAR* 2 (1976): 2-4, 42.

Long live the family name…

In this particular case, Abraham had his servant find a wife for his son Isaac. Abraham likely was not able to physically complete the task himself. He was old. Abraham was 100 when Isaac was born.

Genesis 21:5 Now Abraham was one hundred years old when his son Isaac was born to him.

Genesis 24:1 Now Abraham was old, advanced in age…

Isaac was at least 37 years old when he married. This would make Abraham 137. We get these ages from Scripture and Sarah's age at the time of Isaac's birth. We also know Sarah died before Isaac was married.

Genesis 17:17 Then Abraham fell on his face and laughed, and said in his heart, "Will a child be born to a man one hundred years old? And will <u>Sarah, who is ninety years old</u>, bear *a child?*"

Genesis 23:1 Now Sarah lived <u>one hundred and twenty-seven years</u>; *these were* the years of the life of Sarah.

Abraham was not walking back across the desert to find a wife for his son. His servant was going to find a bride for Isaac.

There is a lesson to be learned in Abraham's servant. The servant is described as **the oldest of his household, who had charge of all that he owned.** This points back to **Genesis 15:2** for the name of the servant.

Genesis 15:2 Abram said, "O Lord God, what will You give me, since I am childless, and the heir of my house is <u>Eliezer</u> of Damascus?"

The servant of Abraham is Eliezer. In the Hebrew language, Eliezer means "God is help". Later in the book of **Exodus**, Moses provides clarification of the meaning of the name.

Exodus 18:4 The other was named Eliezer, for *he said,* "<u>The God of my father was my help</u>, and delivered me from the sword of Pharaoh."

In effect, the Father sends a helper to find the son a bride.

There is a description of how Eliezer is to **take a wife for my son Isaac.** The focus is on the word "take". It is the Hebrew word **laqach.** Remember all the way back in the chapter on defining the word rapture? This is the Hebrew word for the concept of "rapture". **Laqach** is how Enoch was taken.

As a reminder, Strong's Concordance defines **laqach** as: to take, take in the hand, carry along, carry away, take away, or to fetch. Another definition is to take to or for a person, procure, get, take possession of, select, choose, take in marriage, receive, or accept.

Something to think about...hold those thoughts for later.

So what does any of this have to do with Jesus Christ? The Godhead is following the pattern laid out in the Old Testament.

The Father will choose the bride for His Son the groom. And the Father will send a Helper just as Abraham sent a helper. It is stated at least three times, the Father sends the Helper. Jesus bears witness to the statement.

John 14:16-17a And I will ask the Father, and he will give you another Helper, to be with you forever...the Spirit of truth...

John 14:26a But the Helper, the Holy Spirit, whom the Father will send in My name...

John 15:26 But when the Helper comes, whom I will send to you from the Father, the Spirit of truth, who proceeds from the Father, he will bear witness about me.

Other examples include **Luke 24:49** and **Acts 1:4.**

The Greek word for "Helper" is **παρακλετοσ/parakletos.** It can also be translated as: intercessor, consoler, advocate, or comforter. This is a legal term, a defense lawyer in a sense. -Strong's Concordance.

God the Father is ultimately the One who chooses the body or bride of Christ. The Apostle Paul teaches this clearly in the book of **Ephesians.**

Ephesians 1:4 just as He chose us in Him before the foundation of the world, that we would be holy and blameless before Him.

God has always known us and our destiny from before time, **Psalm 139.**

I am sure there are some who will make an argument for free will. Make no mistake. God the Father is reaching out to us. He wants to graft us and have us married into His family. Free will is to be discussed later. And yes we have free will and decision whether or not we choose Jesus Christ. God knows what each individual will choose. That said, Scripture is absolutely clear what God's will is.

2 Peter 3:9 The Lord is not slow to fulfill his promise as some count slowness, but is patient toward you, not wishing that any should perish, but that all should reach repentance.

1 Timothy 2:4 who desires all men to be saved and to come to the knowledge of the truth.

God the Father sends His Helper the Holy Spirit to choose a bride, the body of Christ, for His Son Jesus.

Free Will

The consent and free will choice of the possible bride to be is a consideration. Abraham's servant is clearly concerned about a prospective bride saying "NO". Eliezer did not want to club her over the head and drag her back to the Promised Land against her will.

Genesis 24:5 The servant said to him, "Suppose the woman is not willing to follow me to this land; should I take your son back to the land from where you came?"

Abraham is fine with the bride's refusal. There is only one condition. Do not take Isaac back to Abraham's area of Ur of Chaldea (**Genesis 15:7**). This would be the area of modern day Iraq.

Genesis 24:6 Then Abraham said to him, "Beware that you do not take my son back there!"

It is restated a second time. The woman or the bride can refuse to marry and go. If that is the case, Abraham's top servant was free to go if he chose. Abraham is providing free will and latitude with all parties involved. He is not twisting anybody's arm to do anything.

Genesis 24:8 "But if the woman is not willing to follow you, then you will be free from this my oath; only do not take my son back there."

The text gives the example where Rebecca is asked personally and specifically, do you want to go with me and marry this guy Isaac who you have never seen?

Genesis 24:57 And they said, "We will call the girl and consult her wishes." Then they called Rebekah and said to her, "Will you go with this man?" And she said, "I will go."

Rebekah says "YES" on faith.

http://free.messianicbible.com/feature/ancient-jewish-wedding-customs-and-yeshuas-second-coming/

Follow the pattern. The Holy Spirit is concerned with our free will choice as people. The Spirit of God gives us the choice to refuse Jesus. The Father is okay with us saying "NO" to His Son as a groom, but there is a consequence. But the Father does not want His Son returning to the Earth at this time. It is not time for the Son to return. As Isaac was with his father Abraham, Christ is currently at the right hand of His Father in Heaven.

Romans 8:34 who is the one who condemns? Christ Jesus is He who died, yes, rather who was raised, who is at <u>the right hand of God</u>, who also intercedes for us.

1 Peter 3:22 who is at <u>the right hand of God</u>, having gone into heaven, after angels and authorities and powers had been subjected to Him.

Hebrews 12:2 fixing our eyes on Jesus, the author and perfecter of faith, who for the joy set before Him endured the cross, despising the shame, and has sat down at <u>the right hand of the throne of God</u>.

Acts 2:33 Therefore having been exalted to <u>the right hand of God</u>, and having received from the Father the promise of the Holy Spirit, He has poured forth this which you both see and hear.

If there is no bride for the Son, then the Spirit would be free of His duties within the Godhead according to the pattern.

As believers in Jesus, we trust what we read about Christ. People meet the character of Jesus in the pages of the Bible. It is on faith whether or not we believe the story about Him. This is the test. Do we believe in God? Do we believe what He says?

Hebrews 11:1-2 Now faith is the assurance of *things* hoped for, the conviction of things not seen. For by it the men of old gained approval.

Romans 10:17 So faith *comes* from hearing, and hearing by the word of Christ.

1 John 5:5 Who is the one who overcomes the world, but he who believes that Jesus is the Son of God?

Abraham himself was credited as a "believer" on the issue of faith. He believed in God's promises to come even though he would never see the promises come to pass. This concept is confirmed in the New Testament.

Genesis 15:6 Then he believed in the Lord; and He reckoned it to him as righteousness.

James 2:23 And the Scripture was fulfilled that says, "Abraham believed God, and it was credited to him as righteousness," and he was called a friend of God.

Galatians 3:6 So also, "Abraham believed God, and it was credited to him as righteousness."

See also **Romans 4:3.**

The gospel message of Jesus Christ is an appeal to our free will. We don't have to believe or choose Jesus. We can say no. That does not excuse us from a consequence of our choice. As a friend of mine says, "God is a gentleman." God does not force Himself on us. He does not want a robot. He wants our free will choice to get to know Him. God made us and wants our fellowship. This is an invitation to eternity with God. It is on His terms. He is the Creator. But we can say no.

We are chosen by God. This choice is an appeal to all persons of the Trinity. And we have the free will to say "NO" to God the Father, God the Son, and God the Holy Spirit.

Ketubah

A legal contract is drawn up for the marriage. The contract is called a ketubah. This is the original pre-nuptial agreement. The contract outlines the responsibilities of the groom toward the bride. A Jewish man makes an offer to purchase his bride. The bridal price is also called the mohar. Gifts are given and exchanged including the bride's dowry. In the case of Isaac, Abraham's servant gave gifts to Rebekah and her family.

Genesis 24:53 The servant brought out articles of silver and articles of gold, and garments, and gave them to Rebekah; he also gave precious things to her brother and to her mother.

Rebekah's possessions or dowry were limited when she left for Isaac with Eliezer.

Genesis 24:61 Then Rebekah arose with her maids, and they mounted the camels and followed the man. So the servant took Rebekah and departed.

Remember, Laban watched all of this happen with his sister Rebekah. Laban learned that Abraham had money. He would not forget when Isaac and Rebekah's son Jacob would come later. Jacob's contract with Laban was a series of seven year contracts for his daughters in marriage. See **Genesis chapters 29** and **30**.

What does our contract with Jesus look like? Our contract is effectively the New Covenant. Christ has purchased His bride and the gift is eternal life. The blood of Jesus is the payment of our redemption.

Acts 28:20 Be on guard for yourselves and for all the flock, among which the Holy Spirit has made you overseers, to shepherd the church of God which <u>He purchased with His own blood.</u>

Revelation 5:9 And they sang a new song, saying, "Worthy are You to take the book and to break its seals; for You were slain, and <u>purchased for God with Your blood</u> *men* <u>from every tribe and tongue and people and nation."</u>

1 Peter 1:18-19 knowing that you were not redeemed with perishable things like silver or gold from your futile way of life inherited from your forefathers, but with <u>precious blood</u>, as of a lamb unblemished and spotless, the <u>blood of Christ</u>.

Jesus loves us and promises to continue to love us.

Ephesians 5:25 Husbands, love your wives, just as Christ also loved the church and gave Himself up for her...

Ephesians 5:2 And walk in love, as Christ loved us and gave Himself up for us, a fragrant offering and sacrifice to God.

The gift He is offering is eternal life. In the case of the church, we receive the gift of eternal life from the groom.

Romans 6:23b …but the free gift of God is eternal life in Christ Jesus our Lord.

1 John 2:25 This is the promise which He Himself made to us: eternal life.

John 3:15 so that whoever believes will in Him have eternal life.

As believers, what do we bring to the marriage? What is our dowry? Out of respect to Jesus, we need to behave ourselves. The issue is our response for what Christ has done for us. Believers should live their lives in a Godly manner.

1 Corinthians 6:20 For you have been bought with a price: therefore glorify God in your body.

1 Corinthians 7:23 You were bought at a price; do not become slaves of men.

Romans 12:1 Therefore I urge you, brothers, on account of God's mercy, to offer your bodies as living sacrifices, holy and pleasing to God, which is your spiritual service of worship.

Mikvah

Mikvah is what Christians would call baptism. Mikvah is an immersion into water for spiritual cleansing. This is a Jewish tradition. Prior to the betrothal portion of the marriage, both the groom and the bride are separately cleansed with a mikvah.

http://messianicfellowship.50webs.com/wedding.html

http://free.messianicbible.com/feature/ancient-jewish-wedding-customs-and-yeshuas-second-coming/

Jesus was immersed by John the Baptist in the Jordan River. He has experienced His mikvah.

Matthew 3:13-16 Then Jesus arrived from Galilee at the Jordan *coming* to John, to be baptized by him. But John tried to prevent Him, saying, "I have need to be baptized by You, and do You

come to me?" But Jesus answering said to him, "Permit it at this time; for in this way it is fitting for us to fulfill all righteousness." Then he permitted Him. After being baptized, Jesus came up immediately from the water; and behold, the heavens were opened, and he saw the Spirit of God descending as a dove and lighting on Him...

Believers are to be baptized when they believe in Jesus Christ for their salvation. Baptism comes from the Greek word βαπτισμα/baptisma. The word is transliterated into the English. Per Strong's Concordance it is defined as: a rite of immersion in water as commanded by Christ, by which one after confessing his sins and professing his faith in Christ, having been born again by the Holy Spirit unto a new life, identifies publicly with the fellowship of Christ and the church.

Acts 22:16 Now why do you delay? Get up and be baptized, and wash away your sins, calling on His name.

Galatians 3:27 For all of you who were baptized into Christ have clothed yourselves with Christ.

1 Peter 3:21 Corresponding to that, baptism now saves you-not the removal of dirt from the flesh, but an appeal to God for a good conscience-through the resurrection of Jesus Christ...

Ephesians 5:26 so that He might sanctify her, having cleansed her by the washing of water with the word...

Eyrusin

In the Hebrew language, the word eyrusin means betrothal. The point of the betrothal is for the groom and bride to prepare for the covenant of marriage. This also begins the period of kiddushin in the marriage process. Kiddushin means "sanctification" or "dedication" (definition provided by Wikipedia).

Once in the betrothal, the couple is considered in a legally binding contract. The process could be annulled but it would be considered a divorce. Only the husband had the option of divorce. The prospective bride has no say. An example of grounds for divorce would be the bride's virginity.

http://free.messianicbible.com/feature/ancient-jewish-wedding-customs-and-yeshuas-second-coming/

http://messianicfellowship.50webs.com/wedding.html

The law concerning the matter is noted in **Deuteronomy.**

Deuteronomy 24:1-4 "When a man takes a wife and marries her, and it happens that she finds no favor in his eyes because he has found some <u>indecency</u> in her, and he writes her a certificate of divorce and puts *it* in her hand and sends her out from his house, and she leaves his house and goes and becomes another man's *wife,* and if the latter husband turns against her and writes her a certificate of divorce and puts *it* in her hand and sends her out of his house, or if the latter husband dies who took her to be his wife, *then* her former husband who sent her away is not allowed to take her again to be his wife, since she has been defiled; for that is an abomination before the Lord, and you shall not bring sin on the land which the Lord your God gives you as an inheritance."

The "indecency" in the Hebrew is `**ervah.** It is defined as: nakedness, nudity, shame; pudenda (implying shameful exposure); nakedness of a thing, indecency, improper behavior; figuratively exposed or undefended. -Strong's Concordance.

This is gross sexual immorality. Indecent exposure or adultery could also be included in the behavior.

This was the issue with Joseph and Mary. Joseph could have legally had Mary stoned and executed per the law if she had been with another man and had become pregnant. It appeared Mary had committed adultery during their betrothal. Fortunately, Joseph was visited by an angel in a dream informing him otherwise.

Matthew 1:18-19 Now the birth of Jesus Christ was as follows: when His mother Mary had been <u>betrothed</u> to Joseph, before they came together she was found to be with child by the Holy Spirit. And Joseph her husband, being a righteous man and not wanting to disgrace her, planned to send her away secretly.

As believers in Christ, our lives are a period of sanctification once we believe that Jesus died for our sins. The idea is to be holy and set yourself apart.

1 Thessalonians 4:3 For this is the will of God, your <u>sanctification</u>; that is, that you abstain from sexual immorality…

Romans 6:22 But now having been freed from sin and enslaved to God, you derive your benefit, resulting in <u>sanctification</u>, and the outcome, eternal life.

Hebrews 12:14 Pursue peace with all men, and the <u>sanctification</u> without which no one will see the Lord.

Ηαγιασμοσ/hagiasmos is the Greek word for "sanctification". It can also be translated as: consecration, purification; sanctification of heart and life, separate, holy. -Strong's Concordance

As believers we should prepare ourselves for an eternity with Jesus. Our lives should look different than the culture.

For Jesus' part, He is without sin. Christ has the moral authority. He has no sexual immorality in Him. We have no legal grounds to divorce Him. Yeshua is the perfect husband.

1 John 3:5 You know that He appeared in order to take away sins; and in Him there is no sin.

1 Peter 2:22 He committed no sin, neither was deceit found in his mouth.

2 Corinthians 5:21 He made Him who knew no sin *to be* sin on our behalf, so that we might become the righteousness of God in Him.

Huppah

Next, the couple would come together under the huppah or the marriage canopy. The groom and the bride are coming together in public. They are showing their intention to get married and fulfill their contractual obligation. Tradition has the huppah as a symbol of a new family home.

http://free.messianicbible.com/feature/ancient-jewish-wedding-customs-and-yeshuas-second-coming/

The Hebrew word "huppah" is used three times in the Old Testament. It is translated as "chamber". Two times it used in relation to a bride and groom.

Psalm 19:5 Which is as a bridegroom coming out of his <u>chamber</u>; it rejoices as a strong man to run his course.

Joel 2:16 Gather the people, sanctify the congregation, assemble the elders, gather the children and the nursing infants. Let the bridegroom come out of his room and the bride out of her *bridal* chamber.

Notice in the **Joel** passage, the bride comes from her "huppah" and the groom comes from his "cheder". Cheder is defined as: chamber, room, parlour, innermost or inward part. -Strong's Concordance

The passage in **Joel** suggests the bride and groom will have separate quarters in Heaven. This will be confirmed later by Jesus Himself.

In the **Isaiah** passage below, the term "huppah" is used figuratively as protection of Jerusalem and its inhabitants created by God.

Isaiah 4:5 then the LORD will create over the whole area of Mount Zion and over her assemblies a cloud by day, even smoke, and the brightness of a flaming fire by night; for over all the glory will be a <u>canopy.</u>

Back in the original example in **Genesis**, Isaac took Rebekah into a tent.

Genesis 24:67 Then Isaac brought her into his mother Sarah's tent, and he took Rebekah, and she became his wife, and he loved her; thus Isaac was comforted after his mother's death.

Granted, it was not a huppah but it was a tent or `ohel in the Hebrew. This is a nomadic tent or place of habitation. It is where families lived. `Ohel is also the word used for God's Tabernacle.

Isaac also "took" Rebekah to be his wife. Again, there is our Hebrew word **laqach** (Strong's Concordance). Think Enoch. Be reminded of rapture.

A bride was chosen by a father's helper to be his son's wife. She left her original land and was brought to the home of the son to be his bride. The contract to become groom and bride was established in a tent. Sounding familiar…

Matan

The matan is the bridal gift. The gift is given as reminder. Typically, the groom and bride are separated for about a year per Jewish custom. The gift is a pledge to the bride. It is also a reminder that he will return and take her as his bride.

As the bride of Christ, Jesus has a gift for us. The language written by the Apostle Paul spells this exactly. As believers, we are sealed with the Holy Spirit. The Spirit is a pledge. We will be redeemed.

Ephesians 1:13-14 In Him, you also, after listening to the message of truth, the gospel of your salvation-having also believed, you were sealed in Him with the Holy Spirit of promise, who is given as a <u>pledge</u> of our inheritance, with a view to the redemption of *God's own* possession, to the praise of His glory.

The Holy Spirit is equated with an αρρηαβον/arrhabon in the Greek. The English word is "pledge". **Arrhabon** is a down payment or earnest money. It is defined as: money which in purchases is given as a pledge or downpayment that the full amount will subsequently be paid.

The sealing of the Spirt is the promise of our redemption. We will be changed and freed from the bondage of sin in this body. A glorified body awaits as the bride of Christ.

The birth of the church age began at Pentecost or Shavuot or the Feast of Weeks. These terms are synonymous. This is noted in **Acts 2**.

Acts 2:1-4 When the day of Pentecost had come, they were all together in one place. And suddenly there came from heaven a

noise like a violent rushing wind, and it filled the whole house where they were sitting. And there appeared to them tongues as of fire distributing themselves, and they rested on each one of them. And they were all filled with the Holy Spirit and began to speak with other tongues, as the Spirit was giving them utterance.

Shavuot is often associated with God giving the Torah, the birth of Judaism. Pentecost is often associated with God giving the Holy Spirit, the birth of the church. God chose His appointed holiday to reveal aspects of who He is.

As the bride of Christ, our matan is the Holy Spirit. It is the promise He will come again for us.

Wine

The last activity under the huppah, the couple shares a cup of wine. It symbolizes a blessing for the ketubah. Some see this custom as a term of agreement. By drinking the cup, the bride to be accepts the terms of the marriage. This activity is the completion of the betrothal.

Jesus demonstrated this act with the disciples at the Last Supper. The New Covenant is our cup of wine. This is the fulfillment of Jeremiah's prophecy.

Matthew 26:27-28 And when He had taken a cup and given thanks, He gave *it* to them, saying, "Drink from it, all of you; for this is My blood of the covenant, which is poured out for many for forgiveness of sins."

Believers identify with Christ at communion and remember He died for our sins. The body proclaims the significance of His death. We are entering into covenant with Him when we take His sacrifice for us.

Matthew 26:29 "But I say to you, I will not drink of this fruit of the vine from now on until that day when I drink it new with you in My Father's kingdom."

Another cup will be drunk later at the wedding feast.

Eternal Security

The Trinity is committed to this process. Jesus died for His bride's sin. The Father delivered and gave the Spirit to believers of His Son. And the Spirit is indwelled in believers as a pledge and a promise. Jesus is the example of the perfect husband. Divorce is not an option for a couple of reasons. One, God would violate His character if there was to be a divorce in this relationship. Two, God would separate Himself if there was a divorce. In either case, God would cease to be God. The body of Christ or the church is secure in God the Father, God the Son, and God the Spirit.

Malachi 2:16 For I hate divorce," says the Lord, the God of Israel, "and him who covers his garment with wrong," says the Lord of hosts. "So take heed to your spirit, that you do not deal treacherously."

About One Year...

The couple have a betrothal agreement. The groom and the bride are considered to be married. But the couple lives separately. Sexual relations are not permitted. The best example of this in the Bible is the case of Joseph and Mary. This was the status of the couple. They were considered married. They were living separately. And the text states they had not had sex.

Matthew 1:18-19 Now the birth of Jesus Christ was as follows: when His mother Mary had been betrothed to Joseph, before they came together she was found to be with child by the Holy Spirit. And Joseph her husband, being a righteous man and not wanting to disgrace her, planned to send her away secretly.

As for believers in today's world, we have agreed to be with Christ forever. We are living in separate places. The physical bodies of the church are here on Earth whether we are alive or buried. These bodies are waiting to be transformed and redeemed. Jesus is in Heaven at His Father's house, seated at the right hand.

Groom Responsibility

The groom is to prepare a place for his bride. The father of the groom determines when the home is completed appropriately for his son's bride. The father decides the wedding date. Then, the groom can go get his bride.

John 14:2-3 "In My Father's house are many dwelling places; if it were not so, I would have told you; for I go to prepare a place for you. If I go and prepare a place for you, I will come again and receive you to Myself, that where I am, *there* you may be also."

Tradition has a groom's representative would go before the groom and announce his coming. The Apostle Paul makes the announcement. There will likely be an Earthly announce when the real deal comes in the future.

1 Thessalonians 4:16-17 4:16 For the Lord Himself will descend from heaven with a shout, with the voice of *the* archangel and with the trumpet of God, and the dead in Christ will rise first. Then we who are alive and remain will be caught up together with them in the clouds to meet the Lord in the air, and so we shall always be with the Lord.

Bride Responsibility

The bride should be focused on her preparation. She is to be making wedding garments and maintaining her lamps. These items were kept next to her bed. Mental and physical preparation calls for her to be pure before the groom. Custom has the bride wearing a veil in the public. The veil indicated the bride was taken. She had been purchased for a price. In our case, the blood of the groom.

Ephesians 5:26-27 so that He might sanctify her, having cleansed her by the washing of water with the word, that He might present to Himself the church in all her glory, having no spot or wrinkle or any such thing; but that she would be holy and blameless.

The parable of the 10 virgins in **Matthew 25** models this aspect of the marriage ceremony. So goes the narrative, some virgins were ready and some were not. But that is a study for another day. The focus here is the analogy of the wedding procession.

Tradition states the bride does not know the precise hour or day.

Matthew 25:13 "Be on the alert then, for you do not know the day nor the hour." -Jesus

That's why she keeps her oil lamps at the ready, because she never knows. **Matthew 25:1 "Then the kingdom of heaven will be comparable to ten virgins, who took their lamps and went out to meet the bridegroom..."**

Historically, the groom comes at night around midnight. A shofar or ram's horn is blown. The wedding party would parade through the city on the way to the bride's place.

Matthew 25:6 But at midnight there was a shout, "Behold, the bridegroom! Come out to meet him."

Nissuin

This is the final step of the marriage process. The Hebrew word **"nissuin"** comes from the verb **"naso"**. **Naso** literally means: to lift up or carry. **Nissuin** means: to take.

So the bride is lifted up and taken by the groom.

For the bride and groom, it is back to the huppah or marriage tent. The new couple repeat a blessing over a cup of wine. Vows and promises are exchanged to complete the ceremony. Finally, the bride and groom sign the ketubah or contract in front of a rabbi and two witnesses.

The wedding party ends with the marriage supper. There are seven days of food, drink, and dance. It is a big party. The custom is laid out in the book of **Judges** by Samson.

Judges 14:10-12 Then his father went down to the woman; and Samson made a feast there, for the young men customarily did this. When they saw him, they brought thirty companions to be with him.

Then Samson said to them, "Let me now propound a riddle to you; if you will indeed tell it to me within the seven days of the feast, and find it out, then I will give you thirty linen wraps and thirty changes of clothes.

Revelation 19:9 Then he said to me, "Write, 'Blessed are those who are invited to the marriage supper of the Lamb.'" And he said to me, "These are true words of God."

http://wildolive.co.uk/weddings.htm

And we wait…

Wedding custom and cultural information provided by in this chapter as noted per…

http://free.messianicbible.com/feature/ancient-jewish-wedding-customs-and-yeshuas-second-coming/

http://messianicfellowship.50webs.com/wedding.html

http://wildolive.co.uk/weddings.htm

Chapter 11
Considering the Holy Spirit

The focus is the consideration of the Holy Spirit in regards to the rapture. What are the ramifications to the Holy Spirit if the rapture is anything other than pre tribulation?

There are at least 16 verses in the Bible that proclaim believers in Jesus Christ are indwelled with the Holy Spirit. Below are a few examples.

http://bible.knowing-jesus.com/topics/Indwelling-Of-The-Holy-Spirit

The giving of the Holy Spirit is fulfilled prophecy. The Spirit is coming to Earth.

Ezekiel 36:27 I will put My Spirit within you and cause you to walk in My statutes, and you will be careful to observe My ordinances.

1 Corinthians 3:16 Do you not know that you are a temple of God and that the Spirit of God dwells in you?

2 Timothy 1:14 Guard, through the Holy Spirit who dwells in us, the treasure which has been entrusted to you.

Romans 8:11 But if the Spirit of Him who raised Jesus from the dead dwells in you, He who raised Christ Jesus from the dead will also give life to your mortal bodies through His Spirit who dwells in you.

Since the giving of the Holy Spirit at Pentecost/Shavuot in 33 AD, believers have received the Spirit of God. Today, believers in Jesus Christ have the Holy Spirit. Today, the Spirit resides on planet Earth.

Believers are sealed with the Holy Spirit as well. There are at least 12 verses that state believers are sealed with the Spirit of God. Below are a few examples.

2 Corinthians 2:5 Now He who prepared us for this very purpose is God, who gave to us the Spirit as a pledge.

The pledge is the redemption of our bodies.

Ephesians 4:30 Do not grieve the Holy Spirit of God, by whom you were sealed for the day of redemption.

A believer's body is redeemed and glorified at the resurrection or rapture depending on the body's condition. Our sealing of the Spirit is a statement that we belong to God.

The Spirit is the One who holds back the antichrist. **2 Thessalonians 2:6 And you know what restrains him now, so that in his time he will be revealed.**

The Greek word for "restrains" is **κατεχηο/katecho.** Per Strong's Concordance, it means: to hold back, detain, retain; from going away; to restrain, hinder. The present tense verb indicates the action is continual.

As long as Spirit indwelled believers are on Earth, the evil of the antichrist will be consistently restrained. If the Spirit is still present on the Earth, how can the antichrist be revealed?

If humanity indwelled with the Holy Spirit is present on Earth during the Tribulation (mid or post or whenever), then God the Father is bringing judgment and wrath upon His Spirit. Judgment upon the Spirit would mean sin would be judged twice.

Romans 6:10a For the death that He died, He died to sin <u>once for all</u>...

1 Peter 3:18 For Christ also died for sins <u>once for all</u>, *the* just for *the* unjust, so that He might bring us to God, having been put to death in the flesh, but made alive in the spirit...

Hebrews 10:10 And by that will, we have been sanctified through the sacrifice of the body of Jesus Christ <u>once for all</u>.

There is a Greek word for "once for all". It is **hapax** or **ἅπαξ**. The text says Jesus died it once and it was sufficient.

Was Christ's death the first time not enough? Did Jesus do enough at the cross for sin? Was sin paid for or not?

If the indwelled Spirit comes under wrath or judgment during the Tribulation, Jesus did not do the job at the cross the first time. As believers, we are in Christ. If believers are still on Earth, God would not just be pouring out his wrath on the Holy Spirit but on Christ a second time!

Romans 8:1 There is therefore now no condemnation for those who are in Christ Jesus.

The Spirit would likely argue for a pre tribulation rapture...

###

Thanks for taking the time to purchase and read the book. If you enjoyed the book, please take the time to review at your favorite retailer.

Thanks, Paul

About the Author

Paul Lehr is a Speech Pathologist and home health provider. The majority of his work focuses on swallowing disorders in neurologically impaired patients. He has been a business owner for the past 20 years. Paul earned his BS in Speech Pathology and Audiology from Oklahoma State University. His MA was completed in Speech Pathology at Oklahoma State University.

When Paul's son was born prematurely in 2003, there was lots of support from family and friends. Keeping up with phone calls was too much. So he provided e-mails with updates on health and well-being. In time, his son was healthy and came home. The e-mails stopped but Paul was encouraged to keep writing.

Three years later, Paul was asked to assist in writing a Sunday school curriculum. The lessons were well received by the local body and on the church website. Again, he was encouraged to keep writing. Next, Paul taught a Sunday School class for junior high and high school students. He would share notes with others from the class he was teaching.

Later, a young man at a local church encouraged Paul to start a blog. The website focuses on topical studies such as creation, God's Appointed Holidays and Feasts, the Gospel of Jesus Christ, end times prophecy, ancient Hebrew cultural customs, the Prophet Isaiah, and various topical studies. Three years later, Paul's son told him, "Dad, you need to do updates on how the news is tied to the Bible." The "Trend Update" was born. Since then, traffic on the website doubled in each of the following years. Exposure continues to grow and increase from the previous year.

A friend and fellow Boy Scout father encouraged Paul to start a YouTube channel. His friend thought it was a natural fit considering the content and subscribers from the website. The videos and written posts have been well received. Between the blog and YouTube channel, God's prophetic words have reached over 190 countries.